Secondary Market Price Guide
& Collector Handbook

SECOND EDITION

This publication is *not* affiliated with the Dreamsicles Club™, Cast Art Industries, Inc. or any of their affiliates, subsidiaries, distributors or representatives. Any opinions expressed are solely those of the authors, and do not necessarily reflect those of Cast Art Industries, Inc. The market values listed in this guide are based on compilations of current market trends, but the publisher assumes no liability or responsibility for any loss incurred by users of this guide due to variable market conditions. "Dreamsicles®" is a registered trademark of Cast Art Industries, Inc. All Dreamsicles® artwork is the copyrighted property of Cast Art Industries, Inc., Corona, California.

Managing Editor:	Jeff Mahony	Art Director:	Joe T. Nguyen
	jmahony@checkerbee.com		*jnguyen@checkerbee.com*
Associate Editors:	Melissa A. Bennett	Production Supervisor:	Scott Sierakowski
	Jan Cronan	Staff Artists:	Susan R. Catalfamo
	Gia C. Manalio		Lance Doyle
Contributing Editor:	Mike Micciulla		Kimberly Eastman
Editorial Assistants:	Jennifer Filipek		Ryan Falis
	Nicole LeGard Lenderking		David S. Maloney
	Ren Messina		David Ten Eyck
	Joan C. Wheal		
Research Assistant:	Steven Shinkaruk		

ISBN 1-888914-43-2

CHECKERBEE™ and COLLECTOR'S VALUE GUIDE™ are trademarks of CheckerBee, Inc.
Copyright © by CheckerBee, Inc. 1998.

CheckerBee, Inc.

(formerly Collectors' Publishing)
598 Pomeroy Avenue
Meriden, CT 06450
For all of the latest collectibles news, visit our web site!
www.collectorbee.com

TABLE OF CONTENTS

TABLE OF CONTENTS

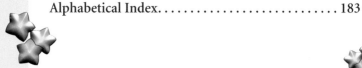

*D*ear Friend,

I am very pleased to present this second edition of the Collector's Value Guide™ to Dreamsicles. This newly revised book will make it even easier to keep track of your favorite Dreamsicles.

During the past year, we have been celebrating five years of fun at the Dreamsicles Club. I'm delighted that, again this year, we are able to provide these informative guides as an extra benefit of membership. As we add new Dreamsicles to the line and others are retired, the *ClubHouse* magazine and your Collector's Value Guide™ will keep you well informed of the latest developments.

Please accept my heartfelt thanks for all your support, kind words and expressions of encouragement. I am honored that so many people find happiness through my little cherubs and animals, and I'm determined to keep making those little smiles for you!

Angel Hugs,

Kristin

Kristin

INTRODUCING THE COLLECTOR'S VALUE GUIDE™

*S*ince their debut in 1991, Dreamsicles – those adorable cherubs created by artist Kristin Haynes – have continually delighted collectors young and old. As the collection continues to expand, the Collector's Value Guide™ provides current information to keep fans up to date. The 1999 Dreamsicles Collector's Value Guide™ is the most comprehensive source of Dreamsicles information (and fun) around!

THE ADVENTURE BEGINS

Take a step into Dreamsicles land and learn about the history of the line. Enter the world of artist Kristin Haynes as she shares family photographs, personal stories and private thoughts in an exclusive interview. See how the Dreamsicles Club celebrated its Fifth Anniversary in 1998, check out all the new releases for 1999, then find out which pieces have the highest value on the secondary market – a great place to start making your wish list!

THE COLLECTOR'S VALUE GUIDE™

Next, journey through the Value Guide with larger-than-ever color photos of Dreamsicles Club pieces, Limited Editions, Cherubs, Heavenly Classics, Dreamsicles Kids and Animals, as well as a host of other Dreamsicles collectibles. Finally, explore the secondary market, learn how to keep your collection looking its best with tips from the experts and find out how to insure your collection.

The Collector's Value Guide™ is filled with everything you need to help make your Dreamsicles collection a dream come true, and is bound to become a treasured companion in your collecting adventure.

COLLECTOR'S
VALUE GUIDE™

*K*ristin Haynes began creating designs for Cast Art's Dreamsicles line in 1991 with the introduction of 29 heartwarming figurines. She continues to charm us with a collection of more than 1,200 pieces, each depicting scenes of child-like innocence and angelic inspiration. These images may take the form of the popular, wide-eyed and winged cherubs, kids in need of divine guidance, animals or holiday personalities in a number of scenes and themes or a variety of companion pieces with the distinctive Kristin "touch."

The handcrafted look that makes Dreamsicles unique features cherubs with wreath halos made of natural dried flowers and pastel ribbon bows. Holiday-themed figurines feature wreaths with tiny red poinsettia and berries accented with red ribbons. A number of animals sport a "poof" of feathers on their heads, but all mirror the angelic eyes and shy smiles of the demure cherubs.

THE ORIGINAL DREAMSICLES

As with most collectibles, Dreamsicles began small in number and simple in design. The "Original 29" pieces included four musicians, six cherubs, seven bunnies and a dozen other animals. These first Dreamsicles family members were born without names but came with descriptive phrases, such as "Large Standing Cow" (later known as "Sweet Cream"). They were also identified with a four digit product code beginning with the number 5.

When Dreamsicles first appeared in retail shops, the line immediately appealed to gift buyers who were searching for the perfect little "something" for Aunt Clara's birthday. For many Dreamsicles collectors, this is how it all began – their first Dreamsicles gift started a collection, either by choice or by chance.

After a successful first year, the introduction of three limited production pieces in 1992 served to enhance the collectibility of the line. Collectors scrambled to find these pieces and turned to the secondary market, where prices began to steadily increase. Subsequent limited editions, as well as early releases and exclusives available at selected outlets, have also fueled interest in the Dreamsicles line.

THE CHERUBS GET A "CLUBHOUSE"

In response to the increasing interest in the cherubs, Cast Art established the Dreamsicles Club in 1993. The club's formation prompted the production of Symbol of Membership and Members-Only pieces available only to Club members.

AS EASY AS ONE, TWO, THREE

1993 was the year that many of the early pieces received names (for example, "Small Sitting Cherub" became "Sitting Pretty") and a new numbering system was adopted. "Dreamsicles the gift line" was becoming "Dreamsicles the collectible" and Cast Art responded with a new, organized identification method for both retailers and customers. The revised numbering system began with a two-letter prefix, followed by a three digit product number. (Cherubs with pastel wreaths received the prefix DC, Holiday Cherubs received DX, etc.) The names and numerical information began appearing on labels affixed to the bottoms of the pieces while the names were engraved on a brass plaques on the Limited Edition pieces.

In January 1997, Cast Art again revised the numbering system for its ever growing Dreamsicles clan. This time, a five-digit numerical code beginning with a "1" was adopted for all Dreamsicles categories. Also, in 1997, the Dreamsicles Day figurines, formerly with the prefix DD, changed to the prefix E.

By 1995, the Dreamsicles family expanded to include "Heavenly Classics," designs of traditional angel images complementing Kristin Haynes' cherubs. The introduction of children with cherubs in the "Dreamsicles and Me" collection set the stage for the "Dreamsicles Kids" debut in 1996. Since then, several mini-series have joined the Dreamsicles family.

HAVE YOU SEEN THIS ONE?

Because Dreamsicles are individually handcrafted, the adage "variety is the spice of life" holds true for this line. The following production variations and redesigns are an interesting footnote for the true Dreamsicles connoisseur.

MISSPELLINGS: The nameplate on the 1995 Special Edition figurine "Poetry in Motion" was initially engraved with the word "Poetry" misspelled as "Potery." About 80 pieces with the error was distributed before it was corrected. Similarly, about 5,000 pieces of the "Rainbow's End" figurine were also produced in 1995 with bottom labels that mistakenly appeared as "Ranibow."

PRODUCTION CHANGES: The prototype of "Springtime Frolic" initially featured a cherub wearing a jaunty straw hat. When the figurine was introduced into the general line in 1994, the hat was replaced with a traditional wreath. "The Good Book" also underwent a production change. The figurine was first produced as an early release in the spring of 1997 with a cherub holding a light tan Bible. When the piece was introduced into the general line as a 1997 mid-year release, the Bible's color was changed to gray.

COLOR CHANGES: In 1997, Cast Art changed the bright, primary colors on 40 existing figurines to softer, pastel hues.

These pieces are marked in the Value Guide section with a palette symbol.

Design, Name & Style Changes: As an early release in 1996, "Making Memories" appeared as number HC381. When it was released to the general line in 1997, the piece retained its name but was re-numbered 10096 and the angel's wings became more sleek in design. Another early release from 1997 experienced an identity crisis when "Together Again" (10246) reappeared in 1998 as "Humpty Dumpty" (10372) with significant design changes, including a sculpted wreath.

Resin Figurines & Sculpted Wreaths: To create more intricately designed Dreamsicles, Cast Art began manufacturing its more detailed figurines out of resin, which is better suited to showcase the complex details than the traditional gypsum material. The resin pieces feature cherubs with sculpted wreaths rather than the dried wreath designs.

The Debut Of Miralite™: The 1998 holiday season ushered in the introduction of Miralite™ – a new high-gloss metallic finish – on selected Halloween and Christmas pieces. The selection of Miralite™ figurines and ornaments included new characters to admire and some old friends sporting a fresh new coat!

BENEFIT FIGURINES

Since 1997, Dreamsicles artist Kristin Haynes has designed special figurines to benefit the American Cancer Society. The 1999 figurine "Relay For Life" is the most recent Dreamsicles designed to benefit the charity, joining "We Are Winning" (1998) and "Daffodil Days" (1997). Cast Art Industries donates a portion of the proceeds from each sale to the fight against cancer.

*K*ristin Haynes, the talented creator behind the Dreamsicles collection, says her biggest influences in her career have been Dr. Seuss, Walt Disney and her mother, watercolorist Abbie Whitney.

Kristin specialized in sculpting at the University of Utah. In 1978, she and husband Scott Haynes moved to southern California where their daughter, Harmony, was born.

Kristin began designing small cherubs and animals to sell at local craft fairs, naming her fledgling company Dicky Ducksprings. After sons Dustin and Patrick were born, she intended to "let up" on sculpting, but the requests for her figurines continued to increase.

To ease the production load, Kristin teamed up with Cast Art Industries of Corona, California. The contract ensured that Kristin's personal style and handmade look would be retained on all pieces. In March 1991, the first 29 figurines were released under the name Dreamsicles.

In 1991, Dreamsicles were recognized as the "Best Selling New Category" by the Gift Creations Concepts group of retailers. By the end of 1992, Dreamsicles were consistently ranked as America's number one gift line in monthly surveys of gift store owners.

Kristin now lives in a farmhouse in Idaho with her family, one dog and three cats. She continues to create her endearing characters, each with a distinctive warmth and charm. She is currently hard at work on a new figurine line called "Love, Kristin." The line will be released in 1999 and will feature "hometown kids doing everyday things."

INTERVIEW WITH KRISTIN HAYNES

*C*heckerBee Publishing recently asked Dreamsicles artist Kristin Haynes to share some of her thoughts about Dreamsicles past, present and future. Here's what she had to say:

CheckerBee: What attracted you to the art of sculpting?

Kristin: My mother is a fine artist and introduced my brothers, sister and me to drawing and painting when we were young. She would buy stacks of typing paper and lots of pencils and we would be entertained for a long time. She probably enjoyed the peace and quiet when we were occupied. She also had a big box of modeling clay that she would bring out and I remember never tiring of creating my own little world of animals and people. Later, in school, I took a lot of drawing and painting classes but, for my own leisure, I would "play with clay." I soon began to realize that I just preferred working in three dimension and the characters I was creating seemed to appeal to people. They were also easy to market when I set out to pursue it as [a source of] income.

CheckerBee: Who have been the most influential people in your career as an artist?

Kristin: My mother, of course, was influential and inspired my interest in art. Later I had some wonderful teachers. Alvin Gittens, who taught in Utah, was one. Once I began selling my art, I learned a lot from other artists when it came to marketing and the art of being in your own business. My father set a great example for his children when it came to dreaming and being a "go-getter." He taught us to never give up on our dreams.

CheckerBee: How did your original company get the name "Dicky Ducksprings?"

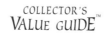

Kristin: The name of my company was simply a sentimental location from my past that I thought sounded like a  unique name for an art biz. We have a family cabin in a canyon outside Salt Lake City. When my father was a little boy and his family would drive up the canyon, they would stop at a spring each time to put water in the radiator since the cars back then would overheat. Every time, my father would wind up falling in the water and they nicknamed him "Dick the Duck." So the spring was then called "Dicky Duck Springs." When we children came along and my father would take us up the canyon to the cabin, we would always stop at this spring for a drink – the car didn't need it – but we always stopped at "Dicky Duck Springs." It was just a great memory and a fun name for my business, although everyone asks if I raise ducks!

CheckerBee: When did you know that you were going to "make it" as an artist?

Kristin: I suppose I knew from a young age that art would always be important to me . . . it was a great way to express myself and also a great escape. When I was in my 20s, I began selling my art and although the money was not abundant, I realized I could make as much as just working a job – and I enjoyed it a lot more.

CheckerBee: Did you have a particular blue-eyed baby in mind when you sculpted your first cherub?

Kristin: I think I always envisioned my own babies when I was creating my cherubs because they were all so cute and cuddly with chubby little cheeks. The blue eyes just always looked so nice with the dried flowers. So that is why they are always blue, no other reason.

CheckerBee: After Cast Art Industries saw samples of your work and decided to produce your pieces, how did the name "Dreamsicles" come about?

Kristin: The name "Dreamsicles" came from the president of Cast Art. I had been calling them "Kristin's Creations." Once Cast Art decided to carry the line, we didn't have much time before the next trade shows so a name had to happen quickly. As I understand it, the name came from some lyrics from a Jimmy Buffett album, although I have yet to hear that song . . . but anyway, it just fit.

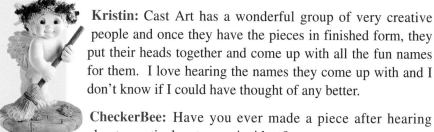

"A number of my pieces are inspired by stories or suggestions from collectors."

CheckerBee: Do you name all of your Dreamsicles pieces yourself or do you ask others for suggestions?

Kristin: Cast Art has a wonderful group of very creative people and once they have the pieces in finished form, they put their heads together and come up with all the fun names for them. I love hearing the names they come up with and I don't know if I could have thought of any better.

CheckerBee: Have you ever made a piece after hearing about a particular story or incident?

Kristin: A number of my pieces are inspired by stories or suggestions from collectors. One of the Club pieces – the little cheerleader – was made in memory of a young teenager that was killed in a car accident. Her mother was given Dreamsicles for comfort and the story she sent me (and pictures of her beautiful daughter) really touched me. It was neat dedicating that piece to her. There is also a cherub using sign language that was suggested by some deaf collectors and, of course, the American Cancer Society pieces. There are quite a few that I did after reading some of the wonderful letters I receive.

CheckerBee: How have your children inspired you?

Kristin: The piece "Chatter Box" was for my daughter (and now, my son). My children have always inspired me and now, just looking through photo albums, I get lots of ideas. Also, a lot of my friends have darling children that I never tire of watching.

CheckerBee: Do you ever get "sculptor's block" and find it difficult to come up with a new idea for a particular piece? Where do you get your inspiration?

Kristin: I have yet to get "sculptor's block." I have so many ideas that each year I just run out of time to do them. The artists at Cast Art are also very helpful and have really cute ideas, so quite often I will work from their sketches. The reps and store owners are wonderful about passing on ideas that their customers have suggested to them.

CheckerBee: You live in a converted farmhouse in rural Idaho. Why did you choose this kind of environment after living in southern California?

Kristin: I grew up near the mountains – hiking and skiing – and missed having that out the back door when we lived in southern California. I also wanted my kids to grow up in that rural environment. It has been just great living in this area. I never tire of watching the squirrels or seeing deer in the yard. It is also a calming and inspiring place and a great place for artists.

CheckerBee: The popularity of angels has grown tremendously in the past few years. Why do you think people are drawn to your cherubs and angels in general?

Kristin: Well, the obvious reasons are always there in regards to the religious population. I sculpted my first cherubs as a Christmas theme when I was selling my art at

"Who doesn't love a cute baby . . . with or without wings?"

shows. Little did I know that people would want to buy them all year round, and I realized all the occasions that angels are appropriate for. I think, also, there is a growing awareness to new age spirituality where angels play a big part. As for the cherubs, I think, "Who doesn't love a cute baby . . . with or without wings?"

CheckerBee: What is your favorite Dreamsicles piece?

Kristin: I cannot say that I have a favorite piece. I think some turned out better than others. I liked "The Flying Lesson" and a lot of the Limited Edition pieces.

CheckerBee: Do you have any collections of your own?

Kristin: I really don't have any collections. I like having one or two pieces from a lot of different lines. I love dolls and teddy bears and have a lot, but almost all are from different artists.

CheckerBee: Do you have any specific design plans for the Dreamsicles line?

Kristin: We are just going to continue to expand the Dreamsicles line. We have a lot of new pieces coming out that have inspirational sayings with them. Also, we are working on a whole circus set.

CheckerBee: What do you think you would be doing today if you had never pursued your interest in art and sculpting?

Kristin: I have no idea what I would be doing if I wasn't pursuing some form of art. Maybe I'd be a brain surgeon – I have a pretty steady hand. (Just kidding!) I enjoy writing – maybe some children's books. I'm glad I chose to do what I'm doing and I think there are a few others that are glad, too.

Kristin greets a young collector wearing a real-life Dreamsicles wreath at the 1998 International Collectibles Exposition in Rosemont, Illinois.

Kristin and Cast Art's Frank Colapinto pose with a happy collector who has just had her piece signed!

*T*his section highlights the new Dreamsicles for Spring 1999. There are 116 exciting new pieces, featuring cherub and animal figurines, the brand new "Angel Hugs" beanbag plush characters, boxes, a cake topper, candle and votive holders, frames, musicals/waterglobes, anniversary plates and a potpourri/candy dish.

DREAMSICLES DAY FIGURINE

Yours Truly . . . Roses are red, violets are blue . . . . A thoughtful cherub ponders over just the right words to use in a poem for his loved one in this exclusive Dreamsicles Day figurine.

LIMITED EDITIONS

Easter Eggspress (LE-5,000) . . . All aboard! The Easter Eggspress will make routine stops throughout the night until everyone's eggs are hidden! You'll want to add your house as a destination for this captivating Limited Edition!

Passage Of Time – Millennium Edition (LE-1999) . . . As the 20th century comes to a close, it's time to make room for a new era. The 1999 cherub passes on the "sands of time" to an eager new keeper in this Dreamsicles Limited Edition figurine.

Stairway To Heaven (LE-10,000) . . . Waiting in the light at the end of the tunnel, these three cherubs want to be the first to greet newcomers at heaven's gate. They bear gifts, welcoming their new friends who will be reunited with loved ones and treated like queens and kings for eternity.

CHRISTMAS LIMITED EDITIONS

Dash Away! . . . Santa and his reindeer have found two eager helpers this Christmas. While Santa delivers his gifts to people everywhere, the cherubs leave their own gifts of love, hope and happiness for mankind.

CHERUBS

Balance Beam . . . This champion gymnast beams as she finishes her routine. We think you'll agree that she's a perfect 10!

Bless This Child . . . A mother gives her child a protective kiss on the head before he heads out into the world for the first time on his own. The child, a picture of innocence, clutches a special gift from his mom to remind him of home.

Bunny Be Mine . . . An unusual couple snuggles together as they drift off to sleep, proving that "everyone needs somebunny to love."

Dreamsicles Garden – Poppy . . . Gardeners may be surprised to find a special treat in their flower pots this year. This adorable little angel has been sown from seeds of love.

Dreamsicles Garden – Sunflower . . . This sunflower will brighten up your day for sure – it comes with a cherub inside!

Easter Colors . . . Someone got a little too carried away with the Easter decorating! At least this cherub's turtle friend will be all ready for the upcoming holiday!

WHAT'S NEW FOR DREAMSICLES

Easter Delivery . . . This inventive pair has found a quick way to spread the holiday spirit! As they fly through the air, they drop eggs for everyone to decorate.

The Easter Story . . . This charming angel and a long-eared friend cuddle together as they learn the true story of Easter in this adorable piece.

The Easter Trail . . . Not many people will get a visit from this Easter "bunny" if he only has one night to hide eggs! Luckily, this "bunny-want-to-be" has a cherub to help in his adventures!

Fast Friends . . . Two cherubs take turns pushing each other around in a wagon. While it's not the fastest way to get around, it sure is the most fun!

A Few Good Men . . . This little marine's salute shows that he is ready to serve his country in the line of duty. While he looks like a tough military man, his smile reveals that he's an angel at heart.

Happy First Birthday . . . It's never too early to introduce your child to the fun of collecting Dreamsicles. This piece is the perfect way to make your Dreamsicles collection a family affair.

Happy Home . . . There's no place like home! This unique "family" spends some quality time together, talking and laughing in the backyard.

Happy Second Birthday . . . The tradition continues as another Dreamsicles (a little bigger this time) arrives to help your toddler celebrate birthday number two.

Happy Third Birthday . . . Birthday number three closes out the Dreamsicles birthday figurine trio, and now your child has a complete set of birthday Dreamsicles to love and cherish forever.

I Love Grandma . . . Won't grandma be surprised when she sees the treat her adorable angel has prepared for her? And she doesn't even have to worry about watering the flowers, as they come inside their own watering can!

I Love You Mom . . . A "green-thumbed" cutie has cultivated a plant specially for mom. This endearing piece is the perfect gift for Mother's Day (or any day).

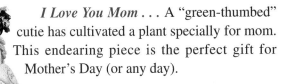

In Full Bloom . . . Miss Morningstar welcomes the new spring season by bringing in a flower bouquet that she collected all by herself! She shyly smiles up at you, offering the lovingly made gift. While the flowers may soon wilt, the affection she brings will last forever.

Jack-In-The-Box . . . Pop! A surprised cherub looks in awe at her toy as a newfound friend pops out to greet her.

Kindergarten Cherub . . . This sweetie selects the perfect apple for his teacher to thank her for teaching him his ABCs, which are proudly displayed beneath him.

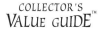

WHAT'S NEW FOR DREAMSICLES

Lady Bug . . . Beauty can be found in the strangest places and when you're least expecting it! This cherub was minding his own business when all of a sudden a new colorful friend flew down to play.

Let's Bee Friends . . . This little cherub shows he wants you to "bee his honey" by offering you a taste of his sweet treat! And he's so sweet himself, who could resist him?

Let's Chat . . . A technologically-advanced Dreamsicles cherub communicates with all of his friends '90s-style via the Internet in this new release.

Mama's Little Helper . . . With a broom in one hand and a rolling pin in the other, this sweet cherub is ready to conquer all the household chores! Now she just has to decide what to do first!

Patches . . . Everyone knows that the best gifts are made, not bought, and this cherub kept that in mind while creating this specially sewn star just for you!

Pep Rally . . . It's the day of the big game and this enthusiastic Dreamsicles cherub sure knows how to show her team spirit. Go team, go!

Reach For The Stars . . . Wearing her graduation cap with pride, this cherub beams as she shows off her brand new diploma. She knows that you can do anything if you set your mind to it.

Reach For The Stars . . . Like her blue-eyed counterpart, this brown-eyed cherub realizes that dreams can come true with a little hard work and persistence.

Relay For Life . . . A cherub runs beside a human friend, encouraging him every step of the way. A portion of the proceeds from this figurine will go to the American Cancer Society, whose symbol is seen on the boy's shirt.

Rub-A-Dub-Dub . . . Puppies need pampering too! "Man's best friend" (or is that *angel's* best friend?) is enjoying every moment of a well-deserved bubble bath from his loving owner.

Sailor Boy . . . Anchors away! Memories of the past and dreams of future adventures fill this little guy's head as he sets off on another voyage. This boatman can't help but smile in anticipation as he gives a big salute before sailing off into the sunset.

Soda-licious! . . . This early release for Spring 1999 features a little angel enjoying a cool, frothy drink after a hard day's work. She must have worked extra hard today; her drink is almost as big as she is!

Soldier Boy . . . This soldier proudly models his army uniform as he gives a stern salute! He hopes he can stand guard on your shelf someday!

Sweet Sixteen . . . Turning 16 is special in itself, but having this well-wishing Dreamsicles cherub by your side as you blow out the candles really puts the icing on the cake!

WHAT'S NEW FOR DREAMSICLES

Tea Time . . . Mom's the guest of honor at today's teatime ceremonies, and won't she be surprised when she sees the specially made teapot with her name right on it!

To Start Your Day . . . This thoughtful little cherub knows that the best way to start your day is to stay in bed with a home cooked meal, so she prepared just that for her beloved mom!

Toy Treasures . . . So many toys to play with and so little time! A tiny cherub looks down in awe at her overflowing toy box, wondering which toy she should play with first!

Treats For Two . . . Looks like this sweetheart has a sweet tooth of his own! Even though he was caught red-handed digging through the desserts, one look at his adorable face makes it impossible to scold this little angel!

Two's Company . . . Practice makes perfect! As they prepare for their big performance, these two budding ballerinas are sure to whirl and twirl their way into your heart.

What Would Jesus Do? . . . This spiritual piece features a cherub deep in thought, looking to the heavens for help as he relaxes on a cloud that expresses his thoughts.

Wild Blue Yonder . . . This young air force recruit can't wait to be flying planes on his own. But for now, he'll have to settle for flying with his own cherubic wings.

Winning Colors . . . Two cherubs work together to get this rainbow prepared for after the storm. It's hard but fun work with the help of a friend!

You Are My Sunshine . . . This little cherub found a friend to help him express his sentiments toward a loved one.

You're My Shining Star . . . This adorable star-covered angel chose a celestial way to express her feelings just for you!

You're So Tweet . . . Love can be expressed in any language, as this bird proves to his seraphim friend. The message is written on the piece, so people who don't speak "bird" can understand the sentiment expressed in this piece.

DREAMSICLES ANIMALS

Mom's Taxi . . . A mother's work is never done! In a piece that every mom can relate to, four baby armadillos cling onto their mother for dear life as she takes them to their individual destinations.

COLLECTIONS & SERIES

Golden Halo Collection . . . Kristin Haynes personally selected eight original cherub designs for this collection, all accented in gold on their floral wreaths and wings: "Golden Best Pals," "Golden Cherub And Child," "Golden Forever Friends," "Golden Heavenly Dreamer," "Golden Make A Wish," "Golden Mischief Maker," "Golden Sitting Pretty" and "Golden Wildflower." The group epitomizes the love and joy brought to people all over the world by Dreamsicles.

WHAT'S NEW FOR DREAMSICLES

Our Daily Blessings . . . Seven Dreamsicles (enough for every day of the week) each come with their own special messages of hope and love: "For God So Loved The World," "A Friend Loveth At All Times," "God Is Love," "In Everything Give Thanks," "It Is More Blessed To Give," "The Lord Is My Shepherd" and "Love One Another."

Love Notes . . . What better way to send a message than through an inspirational angel? Twelve new Dreamsicles cherubs come with a variety of messages for all occasions: "An Angel's Watching Over You," "Babies Are Precious," "Best Pals," "Here's A Hug," "I Believe In You," "I Miss You," "Just For You," "Moms Are a Gift," "Someone Cares," "Thank You," "Thinking Of You" and "You Are My Sunshine."

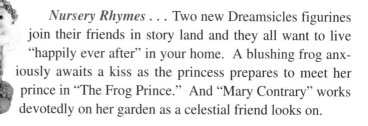

Nursery Rhymes . . . Two new Dreamsicles figurines join their friends in story land and they all want to live "happily ever after" in your home. A blushing frog anxiously awaits a kiss as the princess prepares to meet her prince in "The Frog Prince." And "Mary Contrary" works devotedly on her garden as a celestial friend looks on.

Valentine's Day . . . Ten irresistible cherubs have all been bitten by the "love bug" in these Valentine's Day figurines: "Be My Valentine," "Declaration Of Love," "Key To My Heart," "Kisses For Sale," "Love Poems," "Loves Me, Loves Me Not," "Roses For You," "Unlock My Heart," "Where Love Grows," and "The Woodcarvers."

ANGEL HUGS

Many collectors will enjoy the new "Angel Hugs" collection, a new crew of plush beanbag Dreamsicles that can be squeezed and cuddled. "Angel Hugs" are crafted with satiny wings and embroidered with the winsome Dreamsicles eyes. The collection features three cherubs – "Creampuff," "Cupcake" and "Peaches" – as well as three winged animals – "Bluebeary" the

bear, "Daisy" the cow and "Peanut" the elephant.

OTHER DREAMSICLES COLLECTIBLES

Boxes . . . Seven new Dreamsicles boxes are available for storing your treasures in style: "Dear To My Heart Box," "Morning Glory Birdhouse Box," "Pansies Birdhouse Box," "Pink Roses Birdhouse Box," "Stolen Kiss Box," "Sunflower Birdhouse Box" and "Wedding Cake Box."

Cake Topper . . . This happy couple leaves the chapel together, holding hands as they excitedly start a new life together in bliss. "Cake Topper" makes a perfect wedding day even better for avid Dreamsicles collectors.

Candle & Votive Holders . . . A groom carefully steps over scattered hearts as he carries his blushing bride over the threshold of their new home in "Bride & Groom Candlestick," while a cherub holds an enormous heart-shaped votive in "You Light Up My Life."

WHAT'S NEW FOR DREAMSICLES

Frames . . . Keep the memory of your special day alive with the Dreamsicles "Wedding Bells Frame." And now you can display two of your "special someones" in the "Double Heart" frame.

Musicals . . . These items are a treat for the ears as well as the eyes! In "Rise and Shine," a cherub asleep on a cloud is prodded awake by a friend while "Over The Rainbow" plays in the background. Two festive cherubs decorate for the spring holiday in "The May Pole" as they dance merrily to "Carousel Waltz." "The Melody Makers" features a talented cherub playing "We've Only Just Begun" on his piano while some animal friends join him in song. "Lullaby and Goodnight" plays "Brahms' Lullaby" as a mom rocks her newborn to sleep.

Plates . . . Three new Dreamsicles plates feature a proud wife kissing her husband on the cheek as they share a piece of wedding cake: "25th Anniversary Plate," "50th Anniversary Plate" and "Anniversary Plate."

Potpourri Holder . . . Always the perfect host, the adorable angel in "Potpourri/Candy Dish" offers sweet treats to all her visiting guests.

*D*reamsicles fans have a place they can call "home" with their own Dreamsicles Club. Since the Club was formed in 1993, it has grown to a membership of over 80,000 collectors.

A SPECIAL TREAT

This year, members are in for a treat! Along with the Symbol Of Membership figurine "Share The Magic" and a copy of the 1999 edition of the Collector's Value Guide™ to Dreamsicles, Club members will also receive "Snowflake," a special member of the new Dreamsicles "Angel Hugs" plush toy line. This Members-Only beanbag cherub features a special embroidered heart on its chest and the familiar smile on its face.

LET'S PARTY

In 1998, members had the opportunity to buy two Members-Only figurines: "Summertime Serenade" and the special commemorative piece "Above And Beyond" that celebrates the fifth anniversary of the Dreamsicles Club.

"Summertime Serenade" depicts a cherub reclining in a flower-draped canoe, picking out a few notes on his guitar and singing to the lovebirds that are sitting at his elbow.

"Above And Beyond" was one of the highlights of the Dreamsicles Club Fifth Anniversary celebration held in June 1998 at the International Collectibles Exposition in Rosemont, Illinois. During a video retrospective of the Club's first five years, the figurine was unveiled to more than 300 party goers, 12 of whom were lucky enough to win the figurine in a random drawing. The intricately designed piece features a cherub enjoying a hot air balloon ride in the clouds. What a perfect way for

DREAMSICLES CLUB NEWS

Kristin Haynes to help her fans look "above and beyond" to the future of Dreamsicles collecting!

AND THERE'S MORE

In addition to these great membership benefits, new features are being added to the Dreamsicles Club web site. By entering your Club membership number, you will gain access to a chat room, a "Wish List" page where you can search for your "dream" Dreamsicles and a site where you can e-mail personalized Dreamsicles postcards.

If this sounds like fun and you aren't a Club member, here's what you can do to join:

1. Join online at: *www.dreamsiclesclub.com*

2. Contact the Club at: DREAMSICLES CLUB
   1120 CALIFORNIA AVENUE
   CORONA, CA 91719-3324
   (800) 437-5818

CLUB BENEFITS

For a $27.50 annual fee (or $50 for a two-year membership), Dreamsicles Club members receive:

— Free "Symbol Of Membership" figurine

— Free copy of the 1999 Dreamsicles Collector's Value Guide™

— Subscription to the quarterly *ClubHouse* magazine

— Personalized membership card

— Opportunity to purchase "Members-Only" figurines

— Access to information via a toll-free hot line

— Free exclusive "Angel Hugs" plush beanbag cherub

— New on-line greeting card service

C ast Art retired or suspended from production the following pieces in 1998. These figurines may still be available at retail stores until the existing supply is depleted. Check with your local retailer regarding the availability of these pieces.

1998 RETIREMENTS

Club, Limited Editions & Event Figurines

- ❏ All Aboard! (1998, 10364, *Christmas Limited Edition*)
- ❏ Christmas Eve (1998, 10420, *Christmas Limited Edition*)
- ❏ A Day Of Fun (1998, E9801 *Dreamsicles Day Figurine*)
- ❏ Handmade With Love (1998, 10324, *Limited Edition of 10,000*)
- ❏ Let's Get Together (1998, CD006, *Club Symbol Of Membership*)
- ❏ Time To Dash (1997, 10184, *Christmas Limited Edition*)
- ❏ 'Tis Better To Give (1998, 10421, *Christmas Limited Edition of 5,000*)

Cherubs

- ❏ Best Buddies (1995, DC159)
- ❏ Born This Day (1994, DC230)
- ❏ Brotherhood (1995, DC307)
- ❏ Bubble Bath (1996, DC416)
- ❏ Crossing Guardian (1996, DC422)
- ❏ Daffodil Days (1996, DC343, *American Cancer Society Figurine*)
- ❏ Follow Me (1997, 10050)
- ❏ It's Your Day (1997, 10220)

Cherubs, cont.

- ❏ Love Me Do (1995, DC194)
- ❏ Lyrical Lute (1997, 10169)
- ❏ Mellow Cello (1997, 10170)
- ❏ One World (1995, DC306)
- ❏ Range Rider (1995, DC305)
- ❏ String Serenade (1997, 10168)
- ❏ Sugarfoot (1994, DC167)
- ❏ Taking Aim (1997, DC432)
- ❏ Wishin' On A Star (1993, DC120)
- ❏ Wishing Well (1996, DC423)
- ❏ Wistful Thinking (1995, DC707)

Holiday Cherubs

- ❏ Mall Santa (1996, DX258)

Dreamsicles Kids

- ❏ Free Kittens (1996, DK038)
- ❏ Free Puppies (1996, DK039)
- ❏ Pull Toy (1996, DK027)

Musicals

- ❏ Carousel Ride (1996, DS283)

1998 SUSPENSIONS

Cherubs

❏ Costume Party (1997, 10205)
❏ Easter Morning (1996, DC312)
❏ Go For The Gold (1996, DC315)
❏ Intervention (1996, DC425)
❏ Star Makers (1996, DC344)
❏ Thanks To You (1996, DC316)
❏ Three Wheelin' (1995, DC401)
❏ Topping The Tree (1995, DC407)
❏ Under The Big Top
  (1996, DA251)
❏ A Wing And A Prayer
  (1995, DC410)
❏ Winter Ride (1997, 10177)

Holiday Cherubs

❏ Born This Day (1994, DX230)
❏ Follow Your Star (1996, DX257)
❏ Joyful Gathering (1994, DX231)
❏ Santa's Shop (1997, 10186)
❏ Under The Mistletoe
  (1996, DX253)
❏ Visions Of Sugarplums
  (1996, DX300)

Heavenly Classics

❏ New Beginnings (1997, 10251)
❏ Sounds Of Heaven (1997, 10250)

Dreamsicles Kids

❏ Apple Dumpling (1997, 10059)
❏ Apple Polisher (1997, 10058)
❏ Arctic Pals (1997, 10178)
❏ By The Sea (1997, 10055)
❏ Child's Play (1996, DK018)
❏ Favorite Toy (1997, 10188)
❏ Frosty Friends (1997, 10179)
❏ Kissing Booth (1997, DK042)
❏ Love You, Mom (1996, DK011)
❏ Mush You Huskies (1997, 10180)
❏ Nutcracker Sweet (1997, 10189)
❏ Potty Break (1997, 10056)
❏ Potty Time (1997, 10057)
❏ Sand, Sun And Fun
  (1997, 10054)
❏ Toddlin' Tyke (1996, DK020)

Animals

❏ Baby Jumbo (1997, 10028)
❏ Center Ring (1996, DA250)
❏ Elephant Walk (1996, DA253)
❏ Intermission (1996, DA254)
❏ Opening Night (1996, DA252)
❏ Peanut Gallery (1996, DA256)
❏ Showtime (1996, DA255)
❏ Trunkful Of Love (1997, 10029)

*T*his section showcases the five most valuable pieces in the Dreamsicles collection as determined by their values on the secondary market.

Bundles Of Love *(Heavenly Classics)*
Figurine, HC370
Issued 1996, Suspended 1996
Secondary Market Price: $1,500

The Flying Lesson *(LE-10,000)*
Figurine, DC251
Issued 1993, Retired 1993
Secondary Market Price: $1,100

Happy Landings *(LE-5,000)*
Figurine, 10156
Issued 1997, Retired 1997
Secondary Market Price: $330

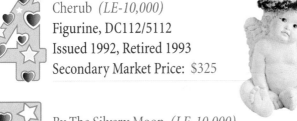

Cherub *(LE-10,000)*
Figurine, DC112/5112
Issued 1992, Retired 1993
Secondary Market Price: $325

By The Silvery Moon *(LE-10,000)*
Figurine, DC253
Issued 1994, Retired 1994
Secondary Market Price: $320

HOW TO USE YOUR COLLECTOR'S VALUE GUIDE™

Cherub (LE-10,000)
DC111 (5111) • 10″
Issued: 1992 • Retired: 1992
Market Value: $120

LIMITED EDITIONS	
Price Paid	Value Of My Collection
1. **51.25**	**120.00**
2.	
3.	
4.	
5.	
6.	
7.	
8.	
9.	
	120.00
PENCIL TOTALS	

1. Locate your piece in the Value Guide. The Value Guide begins with a chronological listing of Dreamsicles Club figurines, Dreamsicles Day figurines, Limited Editions and Christmas Limited Editions. Following this special section are alphabetical listings of Cherubs, Holiday Cherubs, Heavenly Classics, Dreamsicles Kids and Animals (broken down by category, ie., bears, birds, bunnies, etc.). The Value Guide concludes with other Dreamsicles collectibles, such as boxes, eggs, ornaments and more. Handy alphabetical and numerical indexes are located on pages 177 through 191.

2. Find the market value of your Dreamsicles piece. Pieces for which secondary market pricing is not established are listed as "N/E." The market value for each current piece is the 1999 suggested retail price.

3. Record in pencil both the original price that you paid and the current value of the piece in the corresponding box at the bottom of the page.

4. Calculate the total value for the entire page by adding together all of the boxes in each column. Use a pencil so you can change the totals as your Dreamsicles collection grows.

5. Transfer the totals from each page to the "Total Value of My Collection" worksheets beginning on page 163.

6. Add the totals together to determine the overall value of your collection.

SYMBOL KEY

Original **29**	**Color Change**	⁜ AMERICAN CANCER SOCIETY.
ONE OF THE "ORIGINAL 29" DREAMSICLES	PIECE UNDERWENT COLOR CHANGE IN 1997	PIECE BENEFITTING THE AMERICAN CANCER SOCIETY

COLLECTOR'S
VALUE GUIDE™

SPECIAL DREAMSICLES PIECES

This section features exclusive and limited edition pieces. The Dreamsicles Club's 21 pieces include Symbol of Membership figurines, Members-Only figurines and special gift and award pieces. There are six Dreamsicles Day figurines and 27 Limited Edition figurines, which include both general and holiday pieces. The Limited Edition figurines are limited to one year of production unless marked as limited by production quantity.

Dreamsicles Club Symbol Of Membership Figurines

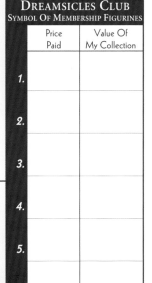

A Star Is Born
CD001 • 4"
Issued: 1993 • Retired: 1993
Market Value: $125

Join The Fun
CD002 • 3"
Issued: 1994 • Retired: 1994
Market Value: $68

Three Cheers
CD003 • 4 ½"
Issued: 1995 • Retired: 1995
Market Value: $60

Star Shower
CD004 • 4 ⅛"
Issued: 1996 • Retired: 1996
Market Value: $45

Free Spirit
CD005 • 4"
Issued: 1997 • Retired: 1997
Market Value: $47

Let's Get Together
CD006 • 3 ¾"
Issued: 1998 • Retired: 1998
Market Value: $42

DREAMSICLES CLUB
SYMBOL OF MEMBERSHIP FIGURINES

	Price Paid	Value Of My Collection
1.		
2.		
3.		
4.		
5.		
6.		

✎ PENCIL TOTALS

1 1999

Share The Magic
CD007 • 3 ¾"
Issued: 1999 • Current
Market Value: $_____

Dreamsicles Club Members-Only Figurines

2 1994

Daydream Believer
CD100 • 4 ⅝"
Issued: 1994 • Retired: 1994
Market Value: $92

3 1994

Makin' A List
CD101 • 5 ⅜"
Issued: 1994 • Retired: 1996
Market Value: $90

4 1995

Town Crier
CD102 • 4 ½"
Issued: 1995 • Retired: 1995
Market Value: $50

5 1995

Snowbound
CD103 • 4"
Issued: 1995 • Retired: 1996
Market Value: $45

DREAMSICLES CLUB
SYMBOL OF MEMBERSHIP FIGURINES

	Price Paid	Value Of My Collection
1.		

DREAMSICLES CLUB
MEMBERS-ONLY FIGURINES

2.		
3.		
4.		
5.		
6.		
7.		
8.		
9.		

✏ **PENCIL TOTALS**

6 1996

Heavenly Flowers
CD104 • 3"
Issued: 1996 • Retired: 1997
Market Value: $45

7 1996

Bee-Friended
CD105 • 4 ¼"
Issued: 1996 • Current
Market Value: $_____

8 1997

Peaceable Kingdom
CD106 • 2 ¼"
Issued: 1997 • Current
Market Value: $_____

9 1997

First Blush (LE-12,500)
CD109 • 8 ½"
Issued: 1997 • Current
Market Value: $_____

(1) 1997

Sweet Tooth
CD110 • 3 ½"
Issued: 1997 • Current
Market Value: $_____

(2) 1998

Summertime Serenade
CD111 • 3 ½"
Issued: 1998 • Current
Market Value: $_____

(3) 1998

Above And Beyond
(5th Anniversary Figurine)
CD112 • 7"
Issued: 1998 • Current
Market Value: $_____

Dreamsicles
Club
Special
Figurines

(4) 1997

Editor's Choice
(Newsletter
Participation Gift)
CD107 • 2 ½"
Issued: 1997 • Current
Market Value: $_____

(5) 1997

Golden Halo ("Good
Samaritan" Award)
CD108 • 2 ½"
Issued: 1997 • Current
Market Value: $_____

(6) 1999

Snowflake
(Membership Gift, Plush)
08008• 8 ½"
Issued: 1999 • Current
Market Value: $_____

DREAMSICLES CLUB
MEMBERS-ONLY FIGURINES

	Price Paid	Value Of My Collection
1.		
2.		
3.		

DREAMSICLES CLUB
SPECIAL FIGURINES

4.		
5.		
6.		

✎ PENCIL TOTALS

Dreamsicles Day Figurines

① 1995

1995 Dreamsicles Day Event Figurine
DC075 • 3 ½"
Issued: 1995 • Retired: 1995
Market Value: $45

② 1996

Glad Tidings
DD100 • 4 ⅛"
Issued: 1996 • Retired: 1996
Market Value: $50

③ 1996

Time To Retire
DD103 • 4 ⅛"
Issued: 1996 • Retired: 1997
Market Value: $35

④ 1997

The Golden Rule
E9701 (DD104) • 4 ⅜"
Issued: 1997 • Retired: 1997
Market Value: $45

⑤ 1998

A Day Of Fun
E9801 • 4"
Issued: 1998 • Retired: 1998
Market Value: $30

⑥ 1999

Yours Truly
E9901 • 3 ⅝"
Issued: 1999 • Current
Market Value: $_____

DREAMSICLES DAY FIGURINES

	Price Paid	Value Of My Collection
1.		
2.		
3.		
4.		
5.		
6.		
✏ **PENCIL TOTALS**		

Limited Editions

(1) 1992

Cherub (LE-10,000)
DC111 (5111) • 10"
Issued: 1992 • Retired: 1992
Market Value: $120

(2) 1992

Cherub (LE-10,000)
DC112 (5112) • 10"
Issued: 1992 • Retired: 1993
Market Value: $325

(3) 1993

**The Flying Lesson
(LE-10,000)**
DC251 • 13" wide
Issued: 1993 • Retired: 1993
Market Value: $1,100

(4) 1993

Teeter Tots (LE-10,000)
DC252 • 6"
Issued: 1993 • Retired: 1993
Market Value: $280

(5) 1994

**By The Silvery Moon
(LE-10,000)**
DC253 • 8 ½"
Issued: 1994 • Retired: 1994
Market Value: $320

(6) 1994

The Recital (LE-10,000)
DC254 • 9 ½" wide
Issued: 1994 • Retired: 1994
Market Value: $250

(7) 1995

Picture Perfect (LE-10,000)
DC255 • 7"
Issued: 1995 • Retired: 1995
Market Value: $150

(8) 1995

**The Dedication
(LE-10,000)**
HC351 (DC351) • 7 ½"
Issued: 1995 • Retired: 1995
Market Value: $200

(9) 1996

**A Child Is Born
(LE-10,000)**
DC256 • 9 ½" wide
Issued: 1996 • Retired: 1996
Market Value: $135

LIMITED EDITIONS

	Price Paid	Value Of My Collection
1.		
2.		
3.		
4.		
5.		
6.		
7.		
8.		
9.		

✎ **PENCIL TOTALS**

1
1996

Heaven's Gate
(LE-15,000, Five Years
Of Dreamsicles)
DC257 • 8 ¾"
Issued: 1996 • Retired: 1996
Market Value: $165

2
1997

Happy Landings
(LE-5,000)
10156 • 7 ½"
Issued: 1997 • Retired: 1997
Market Value: $330

3
1997

Sleigh Bells Ring
(LE-2,500)
10187 • 7"
Issued: 1997 • Retired: 1997
Market Value: $115

4
1997

Cutie Pie
(LE-12,500)
10241 • 8"
Issued: 1997 • Current
Market Value: $_____

5
1998

Handmade With Love
(LE-10,000)
10324 • 5"
Issued: 1998 • Retired: 1998
Market Value: $110

6
1999

Easter Eggspress
(LE-5,000)
10790 • 5 ⅛"
Issued: 1999 • Current
Market Value: $_____

LIMITED EDITIONS

	Price Paid	Value Of My Collection
1.		
2.		
3.		
4.		
5.		
6.		
7.		
8.		

CHRISTMAS
LIMITED EDITIONS

9.		

✏ **PENCIL TOTALS**

7
1999

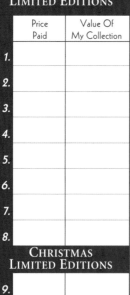

Passage Of Time –
Millennium Edition
(LE-1999)
10671 • 5 ½"
Issued: 1999 • Current
Market Value: $_____

8
1999

Stairway To Heaven
(LE-10,000)
10672 • 7 ¾"
Issued: 1999 • Current
Market Value: $_____

Christmas
Limited
Editions

9
1992

Santa In
Dreamsicle Land
DX247 • 10"
Issued: 1992 • Retired: 1993
Market Value: $305

1 1993

The Finishing Touches
DX248 • 9"
Issued: 1993 • Retired: 1994
Market Value: $180

2 1994

Holiday On Ice
DX249 • 8 ½"
Issued: 1994 • Retired: 1995
Market Value: $155

3 1995

Santa's Kingdom
DX250 • 8 ½" wide
Issued: 1995 • Retired: 1996
Market Value: $125

4 1996

Homeward Bound
DX251 • 9"
Issued: 1996 • Retired: 1997
Market Value: $115

5 1997

Time To Dash
10184 • 6 ¾"
Issued: 1997 • Retired: 1998
Market Value: $95

6 1998

All Aboard!
10364 • 7"
Issued: 1998 • Retired: 1998
Market Value: $100

7 1998

Christmas Eve (LE-5,000)
10420 • 7 ¾"
Issued: 1998 • Retired: 1998
Market Value: $100

8 1998

'Tis Better To Give (LE-5,000)
10421 • 6"
Issued: 1998 • Retired: 1998
Market Value: $70

9 1999

Dash Away!
10791 • 8 ¼"
Issued: 1999 • Current
Market Value: $____

CHRISTMAS LIMITED EDITIONS

	Price Paid	Value Of My Collection
1.		
2.		
3.		
4.		
5.		
6.		
7.		
8.		
9.		
✏ **PENCIL TOTALS**		

CHERUBS

A total of 83 new cherubs have been added to the Dreamsicles lineup, bringing the total to 511 pieces, 337 of which are still available. The cherubs are listed in alphabetical order with the general cherubs first, followed by Birthday Cherubs, Calendar Collectibles, the Gemstone Collection and the new Golden Halo Collection.

---

(1)

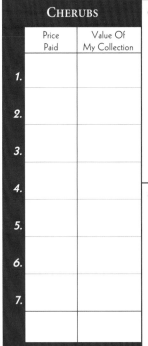

1001 Baby Names
10358 • 5 ½"
Issued: 1998 • Current
Market Value: $_____

(2)

All Better Now
DC246 • 2 ¾"
Issued: 1995 • Suspended: 1997
Market Value: $20

(3)

All My Lovin'
DC313 • 3 ¼"
Issued: 1996 • Current
Market Value: $_____

CHERUBS

	Price Paid	Value Of My Collection
1.		
2.		
3.		
4.		
5.		
6.		
7.		

✏ **PENCIL TOTALS**

(4)

All Star
10165 • 4"
Issued: 1997 • Current
Market Value: $_____

(5)

Among Friends (June)
DC185 • 3 ¾"
Issued: 1994 • Retired: 1995
Market Value: $55

(6)

New!

An Angel's Watching Over You

An Angel's Watching Over You (Love Notes)
10684 • 2 ⅞"
Issued: 1999 • Current
Market Value: $_____

(7)

Anchors Aweigh (Fifth Avenue Exclusive)
10526 • 2 ⅞"
Issued: 1998 • Current
Market Value: $_____

1

Autumn Leaves (October)
DC189 • 5″
Issued: 1994 • Retired: 1995
Market Value: $55

2

New!

**Babies Are Precious
(Love Notes)**
10683 • 2 ⅞″
Issued: 1999 • Current
Market Value: $_____

3

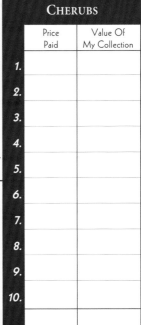

Baby And Me
DC054 • 3″
Issued: 1994 • Suspended: 1997
Market Value: $18

4

Baby Boom
10045 • 3 ½″
Issued: 1997 • Current
Market Value: $_____

5

Baby Boom
10139 • 3 ½″
Issued: 1997 • Current
Market Value: $_____

6

Baby Kisses
DC080 • 2 ½″
Issued: 1995 • Current
Market Value: $_____

7

Baby Love
DC147 • 2 ½″
Issued: 1992 • Retired: 1995
Market Value: $20

8

Baby Steps
DC415 • 3 ⅝″
Issued: 1996 • Suspended: 1997
Market Value: $20

9

Back Packin'
DC346 • 4 ¼″
Issued: 1996 • Current
Market Value: $_____

10

Baked With Love
10262 • 4″
Issued: 1998 • Current
Market Value: $_____

CHERUBS

	Price Paid	Value Of My Collection
1.		
2.		
3.		
4.		
5.		
6.		
7.		
8.		
9.		
10.		

✏ PENCIL TOTALS

CHERUBS

1

New!

Balance Beam
10714 • 3 ¼"
Issued: 1999 • Current
Market Value: $_____

2

The Baptism
10321 • 2 ¾"
Issued: 1998 • Current
Market Value: $_____

3

Bar Mitzvah Boy
DC408 • 4"
Issued: 1995 • Suspended: 1997
Market Value: N/E

4

Bashful
10031 • 4"
Issued: 1997 • Current
Market Value: $_____

5

New!

Be My Valentine
10642 • 4"
Issued: 1999 • Current
Market Value: $_____

6

Bedtime Prayer
DC703 • 3"
Issued: 1995 • Current
Market Value: $_____

CHERUBS

	Price Paid	Value Of My Collection
1.		
2.		
3.		
4.		
5.		
6.		
7.		
8.		
9.		
10.		

✏ PENCIL TOTALS

7

Bee My Honey (Early Release – Spring 1998)
10510 • 4"
Issued: 1998 • Current
Market Value: $_____

8

Berry Cute
DC109 • 3 ⅞"
Issued: 1996 • Current
Market Value: $_____

9

Best Buddies
DC159 • 3 ¾"
Issued: 1995 • Retired: 1998
Market Value: $22

10

Best Friends
DC342 • 6"
Issued: 1996 • Current
Market Value: $_____

Original 29

① **Best Pals**
DC103 (5103) • 4 ¾"
Issued: 1991 • Retired: 1994
Market Value: $45

② *New!*

**Best Pals
(Love Notes)**
10678 • 2 ¾"
Issued: 1999 • Current
Market Value: $_____

③

Bird In Hand
10129 • 3 ½"
Issued: 1997 • Current
Market Value: $_____

④

Birdie And Me
DC056 • 2 ½"
Issued: 1994 • Suspended: 1997
Market Value: $15

⑤

Birthday Fun
10323 • 3 ¾"
Issued: 1998 • Current
Market Value: $_____

⑥

Birthday Party
DC171 • 4 ½"
Issued: 1994 • Suspended: 1995
Market Value: $30

⑦

Birthday Wishes
10166 • 3 ¼"
Issued: 1997 • Current
Market Value: $_____

⑧ *New!*

Bless This Child
10734 • 4 ⅞"
Issued: 1999 • Current
Market Value: $_____

⑨

Bless This Meal
10064 • 2 ¾"
Issued: 1997 • Current
Market Value: $_____

⑩

Bless Us All
DC089 • 2 ⅝"
Issued: 1995 • Current
Market Value: $_____

CHERUBS

	Price Paid	Value Of My Collection
1.		
2.		
3.		
4.		
5.		
6.		
7.		
8.		
9.		
10.		
	PENCIL TOTALS	

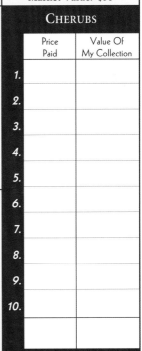

CHERUBS

(1)

Blocks Of Love
10264 • 3 ¾"
Issued: 1998 • Current
Market Value: $_____

(2)

Blowing Bubbles
(Parade Of Gifts Exclusive)
10115 • 3 ⅝"
Issued: 1997 • Current
Market Value: $_____

(3)

Blue Logo Sculpture
DC002 • 6 ½" wide
Issued: 1992 • Retired: 1994
Market Value: $55

(4)

Bluebird On My Shoulder
DC115 • 6"
Issued: 1992 • Retired: 1995
Market Value: $48

(5)

Born This Day
DC230 • 4"
Issued: 1994 • Retired: 1998
Market Value: $32

(6)

Boxful Of Stars
DC224 • 3 ¾"
Issued: 1994 • Suspended: 1995
Market Value: $30

CHERUBS

	Price Paid	Value Of My Collection
1.		
2.		
3.		
4.		
5.		
6.		
7.		
8.		
9.		

✎ PENCIL TOTALS

(7)

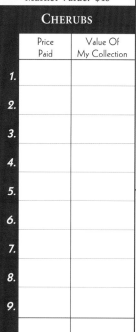

Bright Eyes
DC108 (5108) • 3 ½"
Issued: 1991 • Current
Market Value: $_____

(8)

Brotherhood
DC307 • 4 ½"
Issued: 1995 • Retired: 1998
Market Value: $25

(9)

Brown Baggin'
DC716 • 3"
Issued: 1996 • Suspended: 1997
Market Value: $22

CHERUBS

①

Bubble Bath
DC416 • 5″
Issued: 1996 • Retired: 1998
Market Value: $35

②

Bundle Of Joy
DC142 • 2 ½″
Issued: 1992 • Retired: 1995
Market Value: $20

③

Bunny And Me
DC055 • 2 ⅝″
Issued: 1994 • Suspended: 1997
Market Value: $15

④ *New!*

Bunny Be Mine
10741 • 4″
Issued: 1999 • Current
Market Value: $___

⑤

**Bunny Love
(GCC Exclusive)**
10062 • 3 ½″
Issued: 1997 • Current
Market Value: $___

⑥

Bunny Mine
10068 • 3 ⅜″
Issued: 1997 • Current
Market Value: $___

⑦

Bunny Pal
10342 • 2 ½″
Issued: 1998 • Current
Market Value: $___

⑧

Bunny Power
10067 • 4″
Issued: 1997 • Current
Market Value: $___

⑨ *Color Change*

Burning Love
DC220 • 5″
Issued: 1995 • Suspended: 1997
Market Value: $22

⑩

By The Rules
10520 • 2 ¾″
Issued: 1998 • Current
Market Value: $___

CHERUBS

	Price Paid	Value Of My Collection
1.		
2.		
3.		
4.		
5.		
6.		
7.		
8.		
9.		
10.		

✏ PENCIL TOTALS

1

Caroler #1
DC216 • 6 ½"
Issued: 1992 • Retired: 1995
Market Value: $45

2

Caroler #2
DC217 • 6 ½"
Issued: 1992 • Retired: 1995
Market Value: $45

3

Caroler #3
DC218 • 6 ½"
Issued: 1992 • Retired: 1995
Market Value: $45

4

Carousel
DC174 • 7"
Issued: 1994 • Suspended: 1996
Market Value: $60

5

Catch A Falling Star
DC166 • 4 ½"
Issued: 1993 • Retired: 1997
Market Value: $22

6

Charity
10171 • 2 ⅜"
Issued: 1997 • Current
Market Value: $_____

CHERUBS

	Price Paid	Value Of My Collection
1.		
2.		
3.		
4.		
5.		
6.		
7.		
8.		
9.		

✏ **PENCIL TOTALS**

7

Chatter Box
10039 • 3 ½"
Issued: 1997 • Current
Market Value: $_____

8

Cheerful Givers
(Early Release – Fall 1998)
10624 • 3 ½"
Issued: TBA • Current
Market Value: $____

9

Cherub And Child
DC100 (5100) • 5 ½"
Issued: 1991 • Retired: 1995
Market Value: $60

1

Cherub For All Seasons
(set/4)
DC114 (5114) • 8″
Issued: 1992 • Retired: 1995
Market Value: $85

2

A Child's Prayer
DC145 • 2 ½″
Issued: 1992 • Retired: 1995
Market Value: $15

3 Color Change

A Child's Prayer
DC405 • 4″
Issued: 1995 • Current
Market Value: $_____

4

The Christening
DC300 • 4 ¾″
Issued: 1995 • Suspended: 1997
Market Value: $30

5

Circus Parade
10583 • 4 ⅞″
Issued: 1998 • Current
Market Value: $_____

6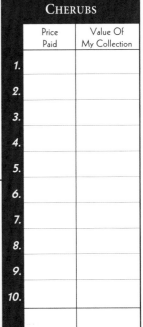

Come To Papa
DC088 • 2 ¼″
Issued: 1995 • Current
Market Value: $_____

7

Corona Centennial
N/A • 3″
Issued: 1996 • Retired: 1996
Market Value: $225

8

Costume Party
10205 • 3 ¾″
Issued: 1997 • Suspended: 1998
Market Value: $20

9

Counting Sheep
DC417 • 5″
Issued: 1996 • Current
Market Value: $_____

10

Cow Pal
10335 • 2 ½″
Issued: 1998 • Current
Market Value: $_____

CHERUBS

CHERUBS

	Price Paid	Value Of My Collection
1.		
2.		
3.		
4.		
5.		
6.		
7.		
8.		
9.		
10.		

✏ PENCIL TOTALS

Dreamsicles® — Value Guide

1 Color Change

Crossing Guardian
DC422 • 5"
Issued: 1996 • Retired: 1998
Market Value: $40

2

Cuddle Blanket
DC153 • 2"
Issued: 1994 • Retired: 1995
Market Value: $20

3

Cuddle Up
DC324 • 2 ¼"
Issued: 1996 • Current
Market Value: $____

4

Cupid's Arrow
DC199 • 5 ¼"
Issued: 1994 • Suspended: 1997
Market Value: $25

5

Cupid's Bow
DC202 (5133) • 7 ½"
Issued: 1992 • Suspended: 1993
Market Value: $115

6

Cut-Out Cutie (Parade Of Gifts Exclusive)
10097 • 4"
Issued: 1997 • Current
Market Value: $____

CHERUBS

	Price Paid	Value Of My Collection
1.		
2.		
3.		
4.		
5.		
6.		
7.		
8.		
9.		

✏ **PENCIL TOTALS**

7

Daddy's Little Angel
10523 • 3 ¼"
Issued: 1998 • Current
Market Value: $____

8 AMERICAN CANCER SOCIETY.

Daffodil Days
DC343 • 3 ½"
Issued: 1996 • Retired 1998
Market Value: $35

9

Daydreamin'
10332 • 6 ½"
Issued: 1998 • Current
Market Value: $____

1

Dear Diary
10162 • 2 ¼"
Issued: 1997 • Current
Market Value: $_____

2 New!

Declaration Of Love
10635 • 3 ⅜"
Issued: 1999 • Current
Market Value: $_____

3

Devotion
10528 • 3"
Issued: 1998 • Current
Market Value: $_____

4

Doggie Pal
10340 • 2 ¼"
Issued: 1998 • Current
Market Value: $_____

5

Don't Rock The Boat
DC404 • 5 ½"
Issued: 1995 • Suspended: 1997
Market Value: $30

6

Double Dip
DC349 • 5"
Issued: 1996 • Current
Market Value: $_____

7

Dream A Little Dream
DC144 • 2 ½"
Issued: 1992 • Retired: 1995
Market Value: $18

8

Dream, Dream, Dream
(Early Release – Fall 1997)
10247 • 2 ⅞"
Issued: TBA • Current
Market Value: $_____

9

Dream On
10365 • 4 ¾"
Issued: 1998 • Current
Market Value: $_____

10

Dream Weaver
10159 • 3 ⅝"
Issued: 1997 • Current
Market Value: $_____

CHERUBS

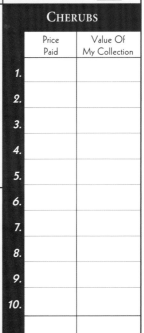

	Price Paid	Value Of My Collection
1.		
2.		
3.		
4.		
5.		
6.		
7.		
8.		
9.		
10.		

✏ **PENCIL TOTALS**

CHERUBS

①

Dreamin' Of You
10030 • 3 ⅛"
Issued: 1997 • Current
Market Value: $_____

②

Dreamsicles Ark Assortment (set/7)
10564 • Various
Issued: 1998 • Current
Market Value: $_____

③

Dreamsicles Garden – Daisy
10551 • 3 ½"
Issued: 1998 • Current
Market Value: $_____

④

Dreamsicles Garden – Lily
10552 • 3 ½"
Issued: 1998 • Current
Market Value: $_____

⑤
New!

Dreamsicles Garden – Poppy
10783 • 3 ⅞"
Issued: 1999 • Current
Market Value: $_____

⑥

Dreamsicles Garden – Rose
10550 • 3 ½"
Issued: 1998 • Current
Market Value: $_____

CHERUBS

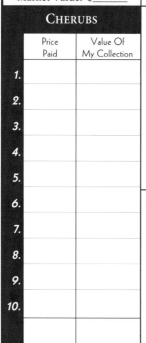

	Price Paid	Value Of My Collection
1.		
2.		
3.		
4.		
5.		
6.		
7.		
8.		
9.		
10.		

✏ PENCIL TOTALS

⑦
New!

Dreamsicles Garden – Sunflower
10782 • 4"
Issued: 1999 • Current
Market Value: $_____

⑧

Dreamsicles Garden – Violet
10549 • 3 ½"
Issued: 1998 • Current
Market Value: $_____

⑨

Dreidel, Dreidel
DC302 • 2 ⅝"
Issued: 1995 • Suspended: 1997
Market Value: $22

⑩

Duckie Pal
10341 • 2 ⅜"
Issued: 1998 • Current
Market Value: $_____

CHERUBS

1

Eager To Please
DC154 • 2"
Issued: 1994 • Retired: 1995
Market Value: $22

2

Easter Artist
10325 • 3 ¾"
Issued: 1998 • Current
Market Value: $_____

3

Easter Basket
10322 • 3"
Issued: 1998 • Current
Market Value: $_____

4 *New!*

Easter Colors
10738 • 3 ⅝"
Issued: 1999 • Current
Market Value: $_____

5 *New!*

Easter Delivery
10739 • 3 ½"
Issued: 1999 • Current
Market Value: $_____

6

Easter Morning
DC312 • 2 ⅞"
Issued: 1996 • Suspended: 1998
Market Value: $20

7 *New!*

The Easter Story
10737 • 3 ½"
Issued: 1999 • Current
Market Value: $_____

8 *New!*

The Easter Trail
10740 • 3 ⅞"
Issued: 1999 • Current
Market Value: $_____

9

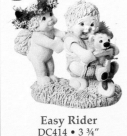

Easy Rider
DC414 • 3 ¾"
Issued: 1996 • Suspended: 1997
Market Value: $20

10

Eggstra Special
10063 • 3 ⅝"
Issued: 1997 • Current
Market Value: $_____

	CHERUBS	
	Price Paid	Value Of My Collection
1.		
2.		
3.		
4.		
5.		
6.		
7.		
8.		
9.		
10.		
	PENCIL TOTALS	

Dreamsicles® — VALUE GUIDE

(1)

Elephant Pal
10344 • 2 ⅜"
Issued: 1998 • Current
Market Value: $_____

(2)

Faith
10527 • 3"
Issued: 1998 • Current
Market Value: $_____

(3) *New!*

Fast Friends
10729 • 3 ¾"
Issued: 1999 • Current
Market Value: $_____

(4)

Feet First
DC320 • 3 ¼"
Issued: 1996 • Suspended: 1997
Market Value: $18

(5)

Felicity
10174 • 2 ½"
Issued: 1997 • Current
Market Value: $_____

(6) *New!*

A Few Good Men
10717 • 3 ¼"
Issued: 1999 • Current
Market Value: $_____

CHERUBS

	Price Paid	Value Of My Collection
1.		
2.		
3.		
4.		
5.		
6.		
7.		
8.		
9.		
10.		

✏ **PENCIL TOTALS**

(7)

Finger Food
DC083 • 2 ¼"
Issued: 1995 • Current
Market Value: $_____

(8)

Fire Drill
10521 • 3"
Issued: 1998 • Current
Market Value: $_____

(9)

First Born
10130 • 4 ⅜"
Issued: 1997 • Current
Market Value: $_____

(10)

First Communion
DC301 • 3 ¾"
Issued: 1995 • Suspended: 1997
Market Value: $28

①

Follow Me
10050 • 4 ¼"
Issued: 1997 • Retired: 1998
Market Value: $30

② New!

For God So Loved the World

**For God So Loved
The World
(Our Daily Blessings)**
10690 • 3 ¼"
Issued: 1999 • Current
Market Value: $____

③ Original **29**

Forever Friends
DC102 (5102) • 4 ½"
Issued: 1991 • Retired: 1994
Market Value: $50

④

FOREVER FRIENDS

Forever Friends
10276 • 3 ¾"
Issued: 1998 • Current
Market Value: $____

⑤ Original **29**

Forever Yours
DC110 (5110) • 10"
Issued: 1991 • Retired: 1995
Market Value: $85

⑥

Forget Me Not
DC325 • 2 ¼"
Issued: 1996 • Current
Market Value: $____

⑦

Forty Winks
DC233 • 3 ½"
Issued: 1995 • Suspended: 1997
Market Value: $25

⑧

**Fountain Treat
(Early Release – Fall 1997)**
10244 • 5"
Issued: TBA • Current
Market Value: $____

⑨

Free Bird
DC234 • 3 ¾"
Issued: 1995 • Suspended: 1997
Market Value: $20

⑩ New!
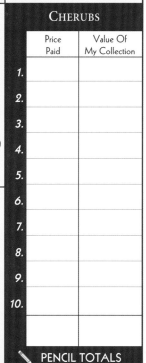

**A Friend Loveth
At All Times
(Our Daily Blessings)**
10688 • 2 ¼"
Issued: 1999 • Current
Market Value: $____

CHERUBS (side tab)

CHERUBS

	Price Paid	Value Of My Collection
1.		
2.		
3.		
4.		
5.		
6.		
7.		
8.		
9.		
10.		

✏ PENCIL TOTALS

(1)

Friendship Cherubs
(set/2)
DC175 • 2″
Issued: 1994 • Current
Market Value: $_____

(2)

New!

The Frog Prince
10765 • 4 ⅜″
Issued: 1999 • Current
Market Value: $____

(3)

From The Heart
10116 • 2 ½″
Issued: 1997 • Current
Market Value: $_____

(4)

Gecko Guava
10005 • 3 ⅝″
Issued: 1996 • Suspended: 1997
Market Value: N/E

(5)

Get Better Soon
DC245 • 3″
Issued: 1995 • Suspended: 1997
Market Value: $18

(6)

Get Well Soon
DC244 • 4″
Issued: 1995 • Retired: 1997
Market Value: $20

CHERUBS

	Price Paid	Value Of My Collection
1.		
2.		
3.		
4.		
5.		
6.		
7.		
8.		
9.		
10.		

✐ **PENCIL TOTALS**

(7)

Get Well Wishes
10320 • 2 ⅞″
Issued: 1998 • Current
Market Value: $_____

(8)

Go For The Gold
DC315 • 3 ⅞″
Issued: 1996 • Suspended: 1998
Market Value: $20

(9)

God Bless America
DC706 • 3 ½″
Issued: 1995 • Suspended: 1997
Market Value: $18

(10)

New!

God Is Love
(Our Daily Blessings)
10689 • 3 ⅜″
Issued: 1999 • Current
Market Value: $_____

1

God's Word
10157 • 3 ⅜"
Issued: 1997 • Current
Market Value: $_____

2

A.

B.

The Good Book
DC361 • 3 ⅜"
Issued: 1997 • Current
Market Value: A. **Gray Bible** – $_____ B. **Tan Bible** – **N/E**

3

Good Shepherd
DC104 • 4"
Issued: 1994 • Suspended: 1996
Market Value: $35

4

Goodness Me
10160 • 2 ⅞"
Issued: 1997 • Current
Market Value: $_____

5

Color Change

The Graduate
DC135 • 5"
Issued: 1994 • Current
Market Value: $_____

6

Graduation Day
DC219 • 4 ¼"
Issued: 1995 • Current
Market Value: $_____

7

Grand Old Flag
DC232 • 3"
Issued: 1995 • Suspended: 1997
Market Value: $18

8

Grandma I Love You
10273 • 3 ¾"
Issued: 1998 • Current
Market Value: $_____

9

Grandma's Or Bust
DC227 • 4"
Issued: 1995 • Current
Market Value: $_____

CHERUBS

	Price Paid	Value Of My Collection
1.		
2.		
3.		
4.		
5.		
6.		
7.		
8.		
9.		

✏ **PENCIL TOTALS**

1

Granny's Cookies
DC228 • 2 ½"
Issued: 1995 • Current
Market Value: $_____

2

Haley
DC321 • 4"
Issued: 1996 • Suspended: 1997
Market Value: $25

3

Hand In Hand
DC431 • 3 ½"
Issued: 1997 • Current
Market Value: $_____

4

Handful Of Hearts
DC204 • 3 ½"
Issued: 1993 • Current
Market Value: $_____

5

Hang Loose
10004 • 3 ⅝"
Issued: 1996 • Suspended: 1997
Market Value: $25

6

Happy Birthday Cherub
DC133 • 4"
Issued: 1994 • Suspended: 1995
Market Value: $30

CHERUBS

	Price Paid	Value Of My Collection
1.		
2.		
3.		
4.		
5.		
6.		
7.		
8.		
9.		
10.		

✏ **PENCIL TOTALS**

7

The Happy Couple
10219 • 6 ¼"
Issued: 1997 • Current
Market Value: $_____

8

Happy Feet
DC164 • 3"
Issued: 1995 • Current
Market Value: $_____

9

New!

Happy First Birthday
10701 • 2 ⅜"
Issued: 1999 • Current
Market Value: $_____

10

Happy Graduate
DC705 • 4 ¼"
Issued: 1995 • Current
Market Value: $_____

(1)

Happy Heart
DC211 • 2 ⅞"
Issued: 1995 • Current
Market Value: $_____

(2) New!

Happy Home
10733 • 3 ⅞"
Issued: 1999 • Current
Market Value: $_____

(3) New!

Happy Second Birthday
10702 • 3"
Issued: 1999 • Current
Market Value: $_____

(4) New!

Happy Third Birthday
10703 • 2 ¾"
Issued: 1999 • Current
Market Value: $_____

(5)

Have A Heart
DC198 • 3 ¼"
Issued: 1994 • Suspended: 1997
Market Value: $22

(6)

Hawaiian Love Song
10003 • 5"
Issued: 1996 • Suspended: 1997
Market Value: $32

(7)

Hear No Evil
10040 • 5 ½"
Issued: 1997 • Current
Market Value: $_____

(8)

Hear No Evil, See No Evil, Speak No Evil (set/3)
10098 • Various
Issued: 1997 • Current
Market Value: $_____

(9)

Heart On A String
10261 • 2 ½"
Issued: 1998 • Current
Market Value: $_____

(10)

Heart Throb
DC193 • 2 ¾"
Issued: 1995 • Current
Market Value: $_____

CHERUBS

CHERUBS

	Price Paid	Value Of My Collection
1.		
2.		
3.		
4.		
5.		
6.		
7.		
8.		
9.		
10.		
✎ PENCIL TOTALS		

(1)

Heart's Desire
DC090 • 2 ½"
Issued: 1995 • Current
Market Value: $_____

(2)

Hearts And Flowers
DC433 • 3 ½"
Issued: 1997 • Current
Market Value: $_____

(3)

Heartstrings
DC197 • 2 ½"
Issued: 1994 • Current
Market Value: $_____

(4)

Heavenly Dreamer
DC106 (5106) • 5 ½"
Issued: 1991 • Retired: 1996
Market Value: $32

(5)

Hello Dolly
DC702 • 3 ½"
Issued: 1995 • Suspended: 1997
Market Value: $20

(6)

Helping Hands (Early Release – Spring 1998)
10506 • 3 ½"
Issued: TBA • Current
Market Value: $_____

CHERUBS

	Price Paid	Value Of My Collection
1.		
2.		
3.		
4.		
5.		
6.		
7.		
8.		
9.		
10.		

✎ **PENCIL TOTALS**

(7) *New!*

Here's A Hug (Love Notes)
10681 • 3"
Issued: 1999 • Current
Market Value: $_____

(8)

Here's Looking At You
DC172 • 4"
Issued: 1994 • Retired: 1995
Market Value: $40

(9)

Here's My Hand
10248 • 4 ¼"
Issued: 1997 • Current
Market Value: $_____

(10)

Here's My Heart
10260 • 2 ½"
Issued: 1998 • Current
Market Value: $_____

1

Hey Diddle Diddle
10373 • 5"
Issued: 1998 • Current
Market Value: $_____

2

Hold Tight
(Cracker Barrel Exclusive)
DC018 • 3 ⅝"
Issued: 1996 • Current
Market Value: $_____

3

Holiday Magic
(December)
DC191 • 5"
Issued: 1994 • Retired: 1995
Market Value: $55

4

Home Sweet Home
10381 • 3 ¾"
Issued: 1998 • Current
Market Value: $_____

5

Hope Has Arrived
(Fifth Avenue Exclusive)
10512 • 4 ½"
Issued: 1998 • Current
Market Value: $_____

6

Housewarming
10525 • 3 ¼"
Issued: 1998 • Current
Market Value: $_____

7

Hugabye Baby
DC701 • 3"
Issued: 1995 • Retired: 1997
Market Value: $18

8

Huge Hugs
10181 • 4 ½"
Issued: 1997 • Current
Market Value: $_____

9

Humility
10173 • 2 ⅝"
Issued: 1997 • Current
Market Value: $_____

10

Humpty Dumpty
10372 • 4 ¼"
Issued: 1998 • Current
Market Value: $_____

CHERUBS

	Price Paid	Value Of My Collection
1.		
2.		
3.		
4.		
5.		
6.		
7.		
8.		
9.		
10.		
✏ PENCIL TOTALS		

Dreamsicles® — VALUE GUIDE

1

Hushaby Baby
DC303 • 3 ¾"
Issued: 1995 • Suspended: 1996
Market Value: $22

2

I.C.E. Figurine
(LE-2,300, I.C.E. Exclusive)
SP001 • 6"
Issued: 1994 • Retired: 1995
Market Value: $185

3

New!

I Believe In You
(Love Notes)
10673 • 2 ¾"
Issued: 1999 • Current
Market Value: $_____

4

I Can Read
DC151 • 2"
Issued: 1994 • Retired: 1995
Market Value: $20

5

New!

I Love Grandma
10710 • 3"
Issued: 1999 • Current
Market Value: $_____

6

I Love Mommy
DC226 • 2 ¾"
Issued: 1995 • Current
Market Value: $_____

CHERUBS

	Price Paid	Value Of My Collection
1.		
2.		
3.		
4.		
5.		
6.		
7.		
8.		
9.		
10.		

✎ **PENCIL TOTALS**

7

I Love You
DC225 • 4 ½"
Issued: 1995 • Current
Market Value: $_____

8

I Love You
10271 • 3 ¾"
Issued: 1998 • Current
Market Value: $_____

9

New!

I Love You Mom
10706 • 3 ¼"
Issued: 1999 • Current
Market Value: $_____

10

New!

I Miss You
(Love Notes)
10677 • 2 ¾"
Issued: 1999 • Current
Market Value: $_____

CHERUBS

1

Ice Dancing
(Early Release – Fall 1997)
10256 • 4″
Issued: 1998 • Current
Market Value: $_____

2 *New!*

In Everything
Give Thanks
(Our Daily Blessings)
10691 • 3 ⅜″
Issued: 1999 • Current
Market Value: $_____

3 *New!*

In Full Bloom
10713 • 5″
Issued: 1999 • Current
Market Value: $_____

4

Integrity
10175 • 2 ⅛″
Issued: 1997 • Current
Market Value: $_____

5 Color Change

Intervention
DC425 • 3 ¾″
Issued: 1996 • Suspended: 1998
Market Value: $20

6

Irish Eyes
DC322 • 2 ⅞″
Issued: 1996 • Current
Market Value: $_____

7 *New!*

It Is More Blessed
To Give
(Our Daily Blessings)
10692 • 3 ⅝″
Issued: 1999 • Current
Market Value: $_____

8

It's Your Birthday
DC304 • 2 ⅞″
Issued: 1995 • Current
Market Value: $_____

9

It's Your Day
10220 • 5″
Issued: 1997 • Retired: 1998
Market Value: $25

10

Jack And The Beanstalk
10376 • 4″
Issued: 1998 • Current
Market Value: $____

CHERUBS

	Price Paid	Value Of My Collection
1.		
2.		
3.		
4.		
5.		
6.		
7.		
8.		
9.		
10.		

✏ PENCIL TOTALS

1
New!

Jack-In-The-Box
10722 • 2 ¾"
Issued: 1999 • Current
Market Value: $_____

2

Joyful Gathering
DC231 • 5"
Issued: 1994 • Suspended: 1997
Market Value: N/E

3
Color Change

Joyful Noise
DC409 • 3 ⅞"
Issued: 1996 • Suspended: 1997
Market Value: $25

4

Jumping Jack
10374 • 4"
Issued: 1998 • Current
Market Value: $_____

5
New!

**Just For You
(Love Notes)**
10679 • 2 ¾"
Issued: 1999 • Current
Market Value: $_____

6

Just Married
10535 • 3 ¾"
Issued: 1998 • Current
Market Value: $_____

CHERUBS

	Price Paid	Value Of My Collection
1.		
2.		
3.		
4.		
5.		
6.		
7.		
8.		
9.		
10.		

✎ PENCIL TOTALS

7
New!

Key To My Heart
10633 • 2 ⅜"
Issued: 1999 • Current
Market Value: $_____

8
New!

Kindergarten Cherub
10724 • 3 ½"
Issued: 1999 • Current
Market Value: $_____

9

King Of The Jungle
10183 • 4 ¼"
Issued: 1997 • Current
Market Value: $_____

10

A Kiss For Momma
DC402 • 3"
Issued: 1995 • Current
Market Value: $_____

CHERUBS

1

A Kiss In Time
DC309 • 4″
Issued: 1995 • Suspended: 1997
Market Value: $32

2

Kiss, Kiss
DC213 • 2″
Issued: 1995 • Current
Market Value: $_____

3 New!

Kisses For Sale
10643 • 3 ⅞″
Issued: 1999 • Current
Market Value: $_____

4

Kitty And Me
DC051 • 3″
Issued: 1994 • Suspended: 1997
Market Value: $15

5

Kitty Pal
10343 • 2 ⅜″
Issued: 1998 • Current
Market Value: $_____

6 New!

Lady Bug
(Early Release – Fall 1998)
10595 • 3 ¼″
Issued: 1999 • Current
Market Value: $_____

7

Lambie Pal
10336 • 2 ⅜″
Issued: 1998 • Current
Market Value: $_____

8

Land Ho!
10043 • 3″
Issued: 1997 • Current
Market Value: $_____

9 New!

Let's Bee Friends
10730 • 2 ¾″
Issued: 1999 • Current
Market Value: $_____

10 New!

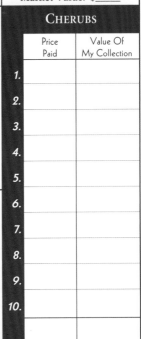

Let's Chat
10735 • 3 ¼″
Issued: 1999 • Current
Market Value: $_____

CHERUBS

	Price Paid	Value Of My Collection
1.		
2.		
3.		
4.		
5.		
6.		
7.		
8.		
9.		
10.		

✏️ **PENCIL TOTALS**

(1)

Let's Eat
(Early Release – Fall 1997)
10252 • 4"
Issued: TBA • Current
Market Value: $_____

(2)

Let's Play Fetch
DC237 • 4 ½"
Issued: 1995 • Suspended: 1997
Market Value: $22

(3)

Life Is Good
DC119 (5119) • 5 ¼"
Issued: 1992 • Retired: 1996
Market Value: $32

(4)

Little Bo Peep
10375 • 3 ⅞"
Issued: 1998 • Current
Market Value: $_____

(5)

Little Cupid
DC212 • 2"
Issued: 1995 • Current
Market Value: $_____

(6)

Little Darlin'
DC146 • 2 ½"
Issued: 1992 • Retired: 1995
Market Value: $20

(7)

Little Leaguer
10366 • 3 ⅛"
Issued: 1998 • Current
Market Value: $_____

(8)

Little One
10033 • 3 ⅞"
Issued: 1997 • Current
Market Value: $_____

(9)

Little Star Chandler
10522 • 3 ¼"
Issued: 1998 • Current
Market Value: $_____

CHERUBS

	Price Paid	Value Of My Collection
1.		
2.		
3.		
4.		
5.		
6.		
7.		
8.		
9.		

PENCIL TOTALS

1

Littlest Angel
DC143 • 2 ½"
Issued: 1992 • Retired: 1995
Market Value: $25

2

Logo Sculpture
DC003 • 7" wide
Issued: 1995 • Current
Market Value: $_____

3

New!

The Lord Is My Shepherd (Our Daily Blessings)
10686 • 3 ¼"
Issued: 1999 • Current
Market Value: $_____

4

Lots Of Love
DC403 • 3"
Issued: 1995 • Current
Market Value: $_____

5

Love In Bloom (May)
DC184 • 5"
Issued: 1994 • Retired: 1995
Market Value: $55

6

Love Letters
DC430 • 3 ¼"
Issued: 1997 • Current
Market Value: $_____

7

Love Me Do
DC194 • 4 ¾"
Issued: 1995 • Retired: 1998
Market Value: $19

8

Love My Bunny
10367 • 4"
Issued: 1998 • Current
Market Value: $_____

9

Love My Kitty
DC130 • 3 ¾"
Issued: 1993 • Retired: 1997
Market Value: $30

10

Love My Lamb
10368 • 4 ½"
Issued: 1998 • Current
Market Value: $_____

CHERUBS

	Price Paid	Value Of My Collection
1.		
2.		
3.		
4.		
5.		
6.		
7.		
8.		
9.		
10.		

✏ **PENCIL TOTALS**

CHERUBS

(1)
Love My Puppy
DC131 • 3 ¾"
Issued: 1993 • Retired: 1997
Market Value: $30

(2)
Love My Teddy
DC132 • 4"
Issued: 1993 • Retired: 1997
Market Value: $30

(3) New!
Love One Another
(Our Daily Blessings)
10687 • 3"
Issued: 1999 • Current
Market Value: $____

(4) New!
Love Poems
10637 • 3 ¼"
Issued: 1999 • Current
Market Value: $____

(5)
Love To Mom
DC717 • 2 ⅜"
Issued: 1997 • Current
Market Value: $____

(6)
Love You Sew
10263 • 3"
Issued: 1998 • Current
Market Value: $____

(7)
Loverly
DC714 • 2 ⅝"
Issued: 1996 • Current
Market Value: $____

(8) New!
Loves Me, Loves Me Not
10644 • 3 ⅝"
Issued: 1999 • Current
Market Value: $____

(9)
Lullaby
DC173 • 10" wide
Issued: 1994 • Suspended: 1997
Market Value: $110

(10)
Lyrical Lute
10169 • 6 ½"
Issued: 1997 • Retired: 1998
Market Value: $18

CHERUBS

	Price Paid	Value Of My Collection
1.		
2.		
3.		
4.		
5.		
6.		
7.		
8.		
9.		
10.		

✎ **PENCIL TOTALS**

1

Make A Wish
DC118 • 5 ½"
Issued: 1992 • Current
Market Value: $____

2

Making A Cake
DC418 • 4 ¼"
Issued: 1996 • Current
Market Value: $____

3 *New!*

Mama's Little Helper
10708 • 4"
Issued: 1999 • Current
Market Value: $____

4 *New!*

Mary Contrary
10766 • 4"
Issued: 1999 • Current
Market Value: $____

5

Matchmaker
10327 • 5 ⅝"
Issued: 1998 • Current
Market Value: $____

6

Me And My Shadow
DC116 • 5 ½"
Issued: 1993 • Retired: 1996
Market Value: $35

7

Mellow Cello
10170 • 9 ½"
Issued: 1997 • Retired: 1998
Market Value: $40

8

Mermaid's Gift
10002 • 4"
Issued: 1996 • Suspended: 1997
Market Value: $45

9 *Original* **29**

Mischief Maker
DC105 (5105) • 5"
Issued: 1991 • Retired: 1996
Market Value: $35

10

Miss Morningstar
DC141 • 7 ¼"
Issued: 1993 • Retired: 1996
Market Value: $50

CHERUBS

	Price Paid	Value Of My Collection
1.		
2.		
3.		
4.		
5.		
6.		
7.		
8.		
9.		
10.		

✏ **PENCIL TOTALS**

1

Mom's Garden
10328 • 4 ½"
Issued: 1998 • Current
Market Value: $_____

2

Mom's The Best
DC428 • 2 ⅜"
Issued: 1997 • Current
Market Value: $_____

3

New!

Moms Are A Gift
(Love Notes)
10682 • 2 ⅞"
Issued: 1999 • Current
Market Value: $_____

4

Monkey Pal
10337 • 2 ⅝"
Issued: 1998 • Current
Market Value: $_____

5

Moon Dance
DC210 • 5 ½"
Issued: 1994 • Retired: 1997
Market Value: $45

6

Moonglow
DC235 • 3 ¾"
Issued: 1995 • Suspended: 1997
Market Value: $18

CHERUBS	
Price Paid	Value Of My Collection
1.	
2.	
3.	
4.	
5.	
6.	
7.	
8.	
9.	
10.	

✎ PENCIL TOTALS

7

Moonstruck
(Early Release – Fall 1997)
10384 (10127) • 3 ⅜"
Issued: 1998 • Current
Market Value: $_____

8

Mother I Love You
10272 • 3 ¾"
Issued: 1998 • Current
Market Value: $_____

9

Mother's Helper
(Early Release – Fall 1997)
10141 • 3 ⅛"
Issued: 1998 • Current
Market Value: $_____

10

Mother-To-Be
10155 • 5 ¾"
Issued: 1997 • Current
Market Value: $_____

CHERUBS

①

Music Makers
10382 • 3 ¼"
Issued: 1998 • Current
Market Value: $_____

②

My First Reader
DC087 • 3"
Issued: 1995 • Current
Market Value: $_____

③

My Funny Valentine
DC201 (5132) • 5 ½"
Issued: 1992 • Suspended: 1993
Market Value: $80

④

My Prayer
DC121 • 5 ½"
Issued: 1992 • Current
Market Value: $_____

⑤

Nature's Bounty (August)
DC187 • 4"
Issued: 1994 • Retired: 1995
Market Value: $55

⑥

Newborn Cherub
DC168 • 3" wide
Issued: 1994 • Suspended: 1996
Market Value: $25

⑦

Newlyweds
10534 • 4 ½"
Issued: 1998 • Current
Market Value: $_____

⑧

'Nite 'Nite
DC238 • 4 ½"
Issued: 1995 • Suspended: 1997
Market Value: $22

⑨

Northern Exposure
DC420 • 5 ½"
Issued: 1996 • Suspended: 1997
Market Value: $55

⑩

Now Give Thanks (November)
DC190 • 4 ¾"
Issued: 1994 • Retired: 1995
Market Value: $55

CHERUBS

	Price Paid	Value Of My Collection
1.		
2.		
3.		
4.		
5.		
6.		
7.		
8.		
9.		
10.		

✏ **PENCIL TOTALS**

CHERUBS

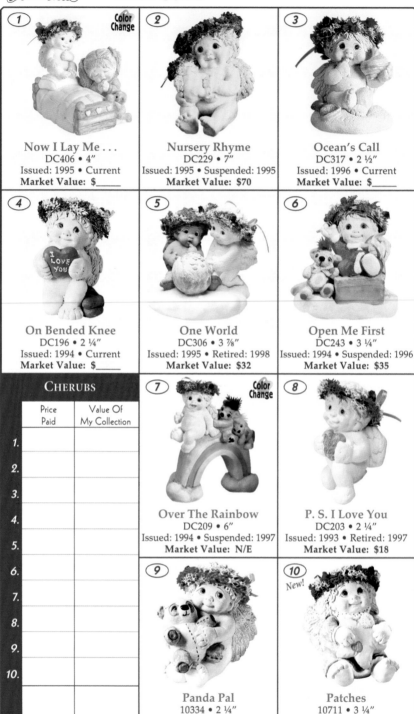

1 Color Change

Now I Lay Me . . .
DC406 • 4"
Issued: 1995 • Current
Market Value: $____

2

Nursery Rhyme
DC229 • 7"
Issued: 1995 • Suspended: 1995
Market Value: $70

3

Ocean's Call
DC317 • 2 ½"
Issued: 1996 • Current
Market Value: $____

4

On Bended Knee
DC196 • 2 ¼"
Issued: 1994 • Current
Market Value: $____

5

One World
DC306 • 3 ⅞"
Issued: 1995 • Retired: 1998
Market Value: $32

6

Open Me First
DC243 • 3 ¼"
Issued: 1994 • Suspended: 1996
Market Value: $35

CHERUBS

	Price Paid	Value Of My Collection
1.		
2.		
3.		
4.		
5.		
6.		
7.		
8.		
9.		
10.		

✎ **PENCIL TOTALS**

7 Color Change

Over The Rainbow
DC209 • 6"
Issued: 1994 • Suspended: 1997
Market Value: N/E

8

P. S. I Love You
DC203 • 2 ¼"
Issued: 1993 • Retired: 1997
Market Value: $18

9

Panda Pal
10334 • 2 ¼"
Issued: 1998 • Current
Market Value: $____

10 New!

Patches
10711 • 3 ¼"
Issued: 1999 • Current
Market Value: $____

(1)

Peaceful Dreams
10331 • 4 ¾"
Issued: 1998 • Current
Market Value: $_____

(2)

Peacemaker
(North Pole City Exclusive)
10257 • 3 ¾"
Issued: 1997 • Current
Market Value: $_____

(3)

**Peacemaker II
"United We Stand"**
(North Pole City Exclusive)
10511 • 4 ⅛"
Issued: 1998 • Current
Market Value: $____

(4)

Penguin Pal
10339 • 2 ⅝"
Issued: 1998 • Current
Market Value: $_____

(5) New!

Pep Rally
10726 • 3 ⅛"
Issued: 1999 • Current
Market Value: $_____

(6)

Piano Lesson
DC413 • 5 ½"
Issued: 1995 • Suspended: 1997
Market Value: $55

(7)

Piece Of My Heart
DC195 • 3"
Issued: 1995 • Current
Market Value: $_____

(8)

Piggy Pal
10345 • 2 ¼"
Issued: 1998 • Current
Market Value: $_____

(9)

Pink Logo Sculpture
DC001 • 6 ½" wide
Issued: 1992 • Retired: 1994
Market Value: $55

(10)

Pint-Sized Parade
DC323 • 3"
Issued: 1996 • Current
Market Value: $_____

CHERUBS

	Price Paid	Value Of My Collection
1.		
2.		
3.		
4.		
5.		
6.		
7.		
8.		
9.		
10.		

✎ PENCIL TOTALS

1

Playground Pony
10319 • 5 ⅜"
Issued: 1998 • Current
Market Value: $_____

2

Playmates
DC020 • 1 ¾"
Issued: 1996 • Current
Market Value: $_____

3

Please Be Mine
10259 • 3 ½"
Issued: 1998 • Current
Market Value: $_____

4

A. POETRY IN MOTION *Special Edition*
B. POTERY IN MOTION *Special Edition*
Poetry In Motion (Special Edition)
DC113 • 5"
Issued: 1995 • Retired: 1997
Market Value: A. "Poetry" – $120 B. "Potery" – N/E

5

Pool Pals (July)
DC186 • 3 ¾"
Issued: 1994 • Retired: 1995
Market Value: $55

CHERUBS

	Price Paid	Value Of My Collection
1.		
2.		
3.		
4.		
5.		
6.		
7.		
8.		
9.		

✏ **PENCIL TOTALS**

6

Pot Of Gold
(Early Release – Fall 1997)
10243 • 4 ⅛"
Issued: TBA • Current
Market Value: $_____

7

Pray For Peace
10356 • 5"
Issued: 1998 • Current
Market Value: $_____

8

Prayer Time
DC148 • 3"
Issued: 1996 • Current
Market Value: $_____

9

Pretty Posies
(Early Release – Fall 1997)
10140 • 3 ⅛"
Issued: 1998 • Current
Market Value: $_____

1

Prima Ballerina
10051 • 4″
Issued: 1997 • Current
Market Value: $____

2

Pumpkin Patch Cherub
DC206 • 3″
Issued: 1993 • Current
Market Value: $____

3

Puppy And Me
DC052 • 3″
Issued: 1994 • Suspended: 1997
Market Value: $15

4

Purr-fect Pals
DC239 • 4 ½″
Issued: 1995 • Suspended: 1997
Market Value: $22

5

Ragamuffin
DC310 • 2 ¼″
Issued: 1995 • Current
Market Value: $____

6

Rainbow Rider
DC236 • 4″
Issued: 1995 • Suspended: 1997
Market Value: $22

7

A.
©1995 Cast Art Industries, Inc.
DC311
Dreamsicles®
"Rainbow's End"
Made in Mexico

B.
©1995 Cast Art Industries, Inc.
DC311
Dreamsicles®
"Rainbow's End"
Made in Mexico

Rainbow's End
DC311 • 2 ¼″
Issued: 1995 • Current
Market Value: A. "Rainbow's" – $____ B. "Rainbow's" – N/E

8

Range Rider
DC305 • 4″
Issued: 1995 • Retired: 1998
Market Value: $22

9

New!

Reach For The Stars
10720 • 4 ¼″
Issued: 1999 • Current
Market Value: $____

CHERUBS

	Price Paid	Value Of My Collection
1.		
2.		
3.		
4.		
5.		
6.		
7.		
8.		
9.		
PENCIL TOTALS		

CHERUBS

1 New!

Reach For The Stars
10721 • 4 ¼"
Issued: 1999 • Current
Market Value: $____

2

Read Me A Story
DC123 • 2 ¾"
Issued: 1995 • Current
Market Value: $____

3

Ready To Roll
DC424 • 4 ¼"
Issued: 1996 • Current
Market Value: $____

4 New! | AMERICAN CANCER SOCIETY.

Relay For Life
10650 • 4 ⅛"
Issued: 1999 • Current
Market Value: $____

5

Ride Like The Wind (March)
DC182 • 4 ½"
Issued: 1994 • Retired: 1995
Market Value: $55

6

Rising Star (Parade Of Gifts Exclusive)
10516 • 4"
Issued: 1998 • Current
Market Value: $____

CHERUBS

	Price Paid	Value Of My Collection
1.		
2.		
3.		
4.		
5.		
6.		
7.		
8.		
9.		
10.		

✏ PENCIL TOTALS

7

Rock-A-Bye
DC158 • 2 ¾"
Issued: 1995 • Current
Market Value: $____

8

Rock Away Rider (Early Release – Fall 1997)
10123 • 3 ⅝"
Issued: TBA • Current
Market Value: $____

9

Rose Garden
DC347 • 4 ¼"
Issued: 1996 • Suspended: 1996
Market Value: $35

10 New!

Roses For You
10636 • 4 ½"
Issued: 1999 • Current
Market Value: $____

① New!

Rub-A-Dub-Dub
(Early Release – Fall 1998)
10495 • 3 ¼"
Issued: 1999 • Current
Market Value: $_____

② New!

Sailor Boy
10715 • 2 ⅞"
Issued: 1999 • Current
Market Value: $_____

③

School Days (September)
DC188 • 4 ½"
Issued: 1994 • Retired: 1995
Market Value: $55

④

Sealed With A Kiss
DC429 • 3 ½"
Issued: 1997 • Current
Market Value: $_____

⑤

Searching For Hope
(Fifth Avenue Exclusive)
DC019 • 4 ¾"
Issued: 1997 • Retired: 1997
Market Value: $155

⑥

Seat Of Honor
DC426 • 4"
Issued: 1996 • Current
Market Value: $_____

⑦

See No Evil
10041 • 5 ½"
Issued: 1997 • Current
Market Value: $_____

⑧

Serenity
10176 • 1 ⅞"
Issued: 1997 • Current
Market Value: $_____

⑨

Share The Fun
DC178 • 3 ½"
Issued: 1994 • Suspended: 1997
Market Value: $25

⑩

Shipmates
10001 • 6"
Issued: 1996 • Suspended: 1997
Market Value: $30

CHERUBS

	Price Paid	Value Of My Collection
1.		
2.		
3.		
4.		
5.		
6.		
7.		
8.		
9.		
10.		

✏ **PENCIL TOTALS**

CHERUBS

1

Side By Side
DC169 • 4 ¾"
Issued: 1994 • Retired: 1995
Market Value: $60

2

Sign Of Love
10158 • 3"
Issued: 1997 • Current
Market Value: $____

3

Signing Figurine
DC074 • 3 ½"
Issued: 1996 • Current
Market Value: $____

4

Sister I Love You
10274 • 3 ¾"
Issued: 1998 • Current
Market Value: $____

5

Sisters
DC427 • 3 ⅛"
Issued: 1997 • Current
Market Value: $____

6 Original **29**

Sitting Pretty
DC101 (5101) • 3 ¾"
Issued: 1991 • Retired: 1996
Market Value: $25

CHERUBS

	Price Paid	Value Of My Collection
1.		
2.		
3.		
4.		
5.		
6.		
7.		
8.		
9.		

✏ **PENCIL TOTALS**

7 Color Change

Skater's Waltz
DC412 • 4 ½"
Issued: 1995 • Suspended: 1997
Market Value: $28

8 Color Change

Sleepover
DC421 • 4 ¾"
Issued: 1996 • Current
Market Value: $____

9

Sleepy Head
DC086 • 2 ¾"
Issued: 1995 • Current
Market Value: $____

1

Sleepyhead
(Early Release – Fall 1997)
10150 • 3 ⅞"
Issued: TBA • Current
Market Value: $_____

2

Sleigh Ride
DC122 • 5"
Issued: 1992 • Suspended: 1995
Market Value: $50

3   Color Change

Small Cherub With
Hanging Ribbon
5104 • 4 ½"
Issued: 1991 • Suspended: 1992
Market Value: $90

4

Snowflake
DC117 • 3 ¼"
Issued: 1994 • Suspended: 1996
Market Value: $22

5

Snuggle Blanket
DC082 • 2 ⅜"
Issued: 1995 • Current
Market Value: $_____

6

Snuggle Buddies
(GCC Exclusive)
DC017 • 5 ½"
Issued: 1996 • Retired: 1996
Market Value: $50

7

Sock Hop
DC222 • 3 ¾"
Issued: 1994 • Suspended: 1995
Market Value: $30

8   New!

Soda-licious! (Early
Release – Spring 1999)
10696 • 3 ⅝"
Issued: TBA • Current
Market Value: $_____

9   New!

Soldier Boy
10716 • 3 ⅜"
Issued: 1999 • Current
Market Value: $_____

10   New!

Someone Cares
(Love Notes)
10674 • 3"
Issued: 1999 • Current
Market Value: $_____

CHERUBS

	Price Paid	Value Of My Collection
1.		
2.		
3.		
4.		
5.		
6.		
7.		
8.		
9.		
10.		

✎ **PENCIL TOTALS**

1

Songbirds
(Early Release – Fall 1997)
10254 • 4″
Issued: 1998 • Current
Market Value: $_____

2

Speak No Evil
10042 • 5 ½″
Issued: 1997 • Current
Market Value: $_____

3

Special Delivery
(February)
DC181 • 5″
Issued: 1994 • Retired: 1995
Market Value: $55

4

Special Occasions Cherub (set/5)
10167 • 6 ¼″
Issued: 1997 • Current
Market Value: $_____

5

Spring Cleaning (Early Release – Spring 1998)
10407 • 4 ½″
Issued: 1998 • Current
Market Value: $_____

6

Springtime Frolic (April)
DC183 • 5″
Issued: 1994 • Retired: 1995
Market Value: $55

7

Stairway To The Stars
DC348 • 5 ⅜″
Issued: 1996 • Suspended: 1996
Market Value: $32

8

Standing Ovation
10163 • 4 ¼″
Issued: 1997 • Current
Market Value: $_____

9

Star Bright
DC084 • 2 ¼″
Issued: 1995 • Current
Market Value: $_____

10

Star Gazers
DC308 • 4″
Issued: 1995 • Suspended: 1997
Market Value: $35

CHERUBS

	Price Paid	Value Of My Collection
1.		
2.		
3.		
4.		
5.		
6.		
7.		
8.		
9.		
10.		

PENCIL TOTALS

1

A Star In One
DC318 • 3 ¼"
Issued: 1996 • Suspended: 1997
Market Value: $25

2

Star Makers
DC344 • 4 ½"
Issued: 1996 • Suspended: 1998
Market Value: $35

3

Star Power
(Early Release – Fall 1997)
10128 • 3 ¾"
Issued: TBA • Suspended: 1997
Market Value: $25

4

Stardust
10385 • 3 ¾"
Issued: 1998 • Current
Market Value: $_____

5

Starkeeping
DC360 • 3 ⅝"
Issued: 1996 • Suspended: 1996
Market Value: $38

6

Starlight, Starbright
DC708 • 2"
Issued: 1995 • Suspended: 1997
Market Value: $15

7

Stolen Kiss
DC162 • 2 ¼"
Issued: 1994 • Current
Market Value: $_____

8

Straight From The Heart
DC314 • 5 ⅞"
Issued: 1996 • Suspended: 1997
Market Value: $22

9

String Serenade
10168 • 6 ¾"
Issued: 1997 • Retired: 1998
Market Value: $32

10

A Stroll In The Park
10357 • 6 ¼"
Issued: 1998 • Current
Market Value: $_____

CHERUBS

	Price Paid	Value Of My Collection
1.		
2.		
3.		
4.		
5.		
6.		
7.		
8.		
9.		
10.		

✏ **PENCIL TOTALS**

1

Sucking My Thumb
DC156 • 2"
Issued: 1994 • Retired: 1995
Market Value: $20

2

Sugar 'N Spice
DC327 • 3 ⅛"
Issued: 1996 • Current
Market Value: $____

3

Color Change

Sugarfoot
DC167 • 5"
Issued: 1994 • Retired: 1998
Market Value: $35

4

Sun Shower
(Early Release – Fall 1997)
10383 (10126) • 3 ½"
Issued: 1998 • Current
Market Value: $____

5

Sunday Stroll
DC400 • 3 ⅞"
Issued: 1995 • Current
Market Value: $____

6

Sunflower
DC221 • 2 ½"
Issued: 1996 • Current
Market Value: $____

CHERUBS

	Price Paid	Value Of My Collection
1.		
2.		
3.		
4.		
5.		
6.		
7.		
8.		
9.		

✏ **PENCIL TOTALS**

7

Super Star
DC704 • 6"
Issued: 1995 • Suspended: 1997
Market Value: $25

8

Surprise Gift
DC152 • 2"
Issued: 1994 • Retired: 1995
Market Value: $18

9

Swan Lake
DC163 • 3 ½"
Issued: 1995 • Current
Market Value: $____

(1)

Sweet Bouquet
DC081 • 2 ¼"
Issued: 1995 • Current
Market Value: $_____

(2)

Sweet Chariot
DC345 • 4"
Issued: 1996 • Current
Market Value: $_____

(3) Color Change

Sweet Charity
DC411 • 4 ¼"
Issued: 1995 • Suspended: 1997
Market Value: $28

(4)

Sweet Dreams
DC125 • 11"
Issued: 1993 • Retired: 1995
Market Value: $70

(5)

Sweet Gingerbread
DC223 • 3 ¾"
Issued: 1994 • Suspended: 1995
Market Value: $30

(6)

Sweet Pea
10038 • 3 ¾"
Issued: 1997 • Current
Market Value: $_____

(7)

Sweet Sentiments (Early Release – Spring 1998
10406 • 3 ⅝"
Issued: TBA • Current
Market Value: $_____

(8) New!

Sweet Sixteen
10731 • 3 ⅞"
Issued: 1999 • Current
Market Value: $_____

(9)

Sweethearts
DC200 • 6"
Issued: 1994 • Suspended: 1997
Market Value: $40

(10)

Sweetums
10161 • 3"
Issued: 1997 • Current
Market Value: $_____

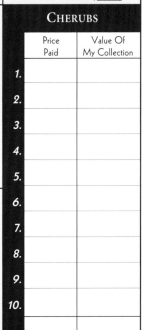

CHERUBS

	Price Paid	Value Of My Collection
1.		
2.		
3.		
4.		
5.		
6.		
7.		
8.		
9.		
10.		
✏ PENCIL TOTALS		

CHERUBS

1

Swimming For Hope
(Fifth Avenue Exclusive)
DC016 • 5"
Issued: 1996 • Retired: 1996
Market Value: $130

2 Color Change

Swing On A Star
DC208 • 5 ½"
Issued: 1994 • Suspended: 1997
Market Value: $40

3

Swingtime
10044 • 4"
Issued: 1997 • Current
Market Value: $_____

4

Taking Aim
DC432 • 6" wide
Issued: 1997 • Retired: 1998
Market Value: $28

5

Tea Party
(GCC Exclusive)
DC015 • 3"
Issued: 1996 • Retired: 1996
Market Value: $55

6 New!

Tea Time
10705 • 3 ⅛"
Issued: 1999 • Current
Market Value: $_____

CHERUBS

	Price Paid	Value Of My Collection
1.		
2.		
3.		
4.		
5.		
6.		
7.		
8.		
9.		
10.		

✏ **PENCIL TOTALS**

7

Teacher's Pet
DC124 • 5"
Issued: 1993 • Retired: 1997
Market Value: $35

8

Team Player
10164 • 3 ¾"
Issued: 1997 • Current
Market Value: $____

9

Teddy And Me
DC053 • 3"
Issued: 1994 • Suspended: 1997
Market Value: $20

10

Tender Loving Care
DC247 • 3 ¼"
Issued: 1995 • Suspended: 1997
Market Value: $20

1 *New!*

Thank You
(Love Notes)
10675 • 3"
Issued: 1999 • Current
Market Value: $_____

2

Thanks To You
DC316 • 3 ⅜"
Issued: 1996 • Suspended: 1998
Market Value: $20

3

Thanksgiving Cherubs
DC207 • 3 ¼"
Issued: 1994 • Current
Market Value: $_____

4

Thinking Of You
DC129 • 9"
Issued: 1993 • Retired: 1997
Market Value: $70

5 *New!*

Thinking Of You
(Love Notes)
10676 • 2 ¾"
Issued: 1999 • Current
Market Value: $_____

6

Three Amigos
DC179 • 3 ¼"
Issued: 1994 • Suspended: 1997
Market Value: $20

7

Three Wheelin'
DC401 • 4"
Issued: 1995 • Suspended: 1998
Market Value: N/E

8

Tiger By The Tail
10182 • 4 ¼"
Issued: 1997 • Current
Market Value: $_____

9

Tiny Dancer
DC165 • 4 ½"
Issued: 1993 • Retired: 1997
Market Value: $25

10 *New!*

To Start Your Day
10707 • 4 ⅜"
Issued: 1999 • Current
Market Value: $_____

CHERUBS

	Price Paid	Value Of My Collection
1.		
2.		
3.		
4.		
5.		
6.		
7.		
8.		
9.		
10.		
PENCIL TOTALS		

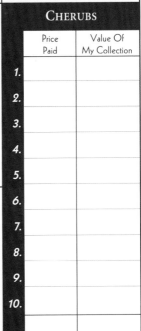

CHERUBS

1

Together Again
(Early Release – Fall 1997)
10246 • 4"
Issued: TBA • Suspended: 1997
Market Value: $18

2

Color Change

Topping The Tree
DC407 • 4"
Issued: 1995 • Suspended: 1998
Market Value: $32

3

New!

Toy Treasures
(Early Release – Fall 1998)
10514 • 3 ⅝"
Issued: 1999 • Current
Market Value: $____

4

New!

Treats For Two
10699 • 3 ½"
Issued: 1999 • Current
Market Value: $____

5

Twice The Fun
(Early Release – Fall 1998)
10505 • 4 ¼"
Issued: TBA • Current
Market Value: $____

6

Twinkle Toes
DC091 • 2 ¼"
Issued: 1995 • Current
Market Value: $____

CHERUBS

	Price Paid	Value Of My Collection
1.		
2.		
3.		
4.		
5.		
6.		
7.		
8.		
9.		
10.		

✏ **PENCIL TOTALS**

7

Twinkle, Twinkle
DC700 • 3 ½"
Issued: 1995 • Retired: 1997
Market Value: $22

8

New!

Two's Company
10727 • 3 ¾"
Issued: 1999 • Current
Market Value: $____

9

Twosome
DC149 • 5"
Issued: 1996 • Suspended: 1997
Market Value: $30

10

Under The Big Top
DA251 • 5"
Issued: 1996 • Suspended: 1998
Market Value: $30

1

Unicorn Pal
10338 • 2 ½"
Issued: 1998 • Current
Market Value: $____

2

New!

Unlock My Heart
10632 • 2 ⅜"
Issued: 1999 • Current
Market Value: $____

3

Up All Night
DC155 • 2"
Issued: 1994 • Retired: 1995
Market Value: $18

4

Upsy Daisy!
DC085 • 2 ⅛"
Issued: 1995 • Current
Market Value: $____

5

Vitality
10172 • 2 ¼"
Issued: 1997 • Current
Market Value: $____

6

AMERICAN CANCER SOCIETY.

We Are Winning
10380 • 3 ⅝"
Issued: 1998 • Current
Market Value: $____

7

We're Best Friends
DC715 • 6"
Issued: 1996 • Suspended: 1997
Market Value: $30

8

The Wedding March
10121 • 6"
Issued: 1997 • Current
Market Value: $____

9

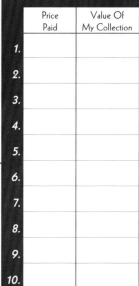

Wedding Rehearsal
DC134 • 5"
Issued: 1994 • Current
Market Value: $____

10

New!

What Would Jesus Do?
10725 • 3 ¼"
Issued: 1999 • Current
Market Value: $____

CHERUBS

	Price Paid	Value Of My Collection
1.		
2.		
3.		
4.		
5.		
6.		
7.		
8.		
9.		
10.		
✏ PENCIL TOTALS		

1 New!

Where Love Grows
10638 • 3 ¾"
Issued: 1999 • Current
Market Value: $____

2 New!

Wild Blue Yonder
10718 • 3 ⅛"
Issued: 1999 • Current
Market Value: $____

3

Wildflower
DC107 (5107) • 3 ½"
Issued: 1991 • Retired: 1996
Market Value: $25

4

Windy City (European Imports Exclusive)
10151 • 5 ½"
Issued: 1997 • Current
Market Value: $____

5 Color Change

A Wing And A Prayer
DC410 • 4 ¾"
Issued: 1995 • Suspended: 1998
Market Value: N/E

6

Winger
DC319 • 3 ¼"
Issued: 1996 • Suspended: 1997
Market Value: $18

CHERUBS

	Price Paid	Value Of My Collection
1.		
2.		
3.		
4.		
5.		
6.		
7.		
8.		
9.		

✎ PENCIL TOTALS

7 New!

Winning Colors
(Early Release – Fall 1998)
10515 • 4"
Issued: 1999 • Current
Market Value: $____

8

Winter Ride
10177 • 5 ¾"
Issued: 1997 • Suspended: 1998
Market Value: $22

9

Winter Wonderland
(January)
DC180 • 5 ½"
Issued: 1994 • Retired: 1995
Market Value: $55

(1)

Wish You Were Here
10075 • 4 ⅛"
Issued: 1997 • Current
Market Value: $____

(2)

Wishin' On A Star
DC120 • 4 ¼"
Issued: 1993 • Retired: 1998
Market Value: $20

(3)

Wishing 'N Hoping
DC328 • 3 ¼"
Issued: 1996 • Current
Market Value: $____

(4) Color Change

Wishing Well
DC423 • 6 ¼"
Issued: 1996 • Retired: 1998
Market Value: $40

(5)

Wistful Thinking
DC707 • 2"
Issued: 1995 • Retired: 1998
Market Value: $20

(6) New!

The Woodcarvers
10631 • 4"
Issued: 1999 • Current
Market Value: $____

CHERUBS

(7) New!

You Are My Sunshine
(Love Notes)
10680 • 2 ¾"
Issued: 1999 • Current
Market Value: $____

(8) New!

You Are My Sunshine
10728 • 3 ½"
Issued: 1999 • Current
Market Value: $____

(9) New!

You're My Shining Star
10712 • 5 ½"
Issued: 1999 • Current
Market Value: $____

(10) New!

You're So Tweet
10723 • 3 ¼"
Issued: 1999 • Current
Market Value: $____

	Price Paid	Value Of My Collection
1.		
2.		
3.		
4.		
5.		
6.		
7.		
8.		
9.		
10.		
✏ PENCIL TOTALS		

CHERUBS

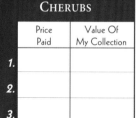

You're Special
10275 • 3 ¾"
Issued: 1998 • Current
Market Value: $_____

You've Got A Friend
DC170 • 6"
Issued: 1994 • Suspended: 1997
Market Value: $45

Young Love
DC214 • 2"
Issued: 1995 • Current
Market Value: $_____

Number Zero
DC071 • 3"
Issued: 1996 • Current
Market Value: $_____

First Birthday
DC061 • 2 ½"
Issued: 1995 • Current
Market Value: $_____

Second Birthday
DC062 • 2 ½"
Issued: 1995 • Current
Market Value: $_____

CHERUBS

	Price Paid	Value Of My Collection
1.		
2.		
3.		

CHERUBS
BIRTHDAY CHERUBS

4.		
5.		
6.		
7.		
8.		
9.		

✏ **PENCIL TOTALS**

Third Birthday
DC063 • 2 ½"
Issued: 1995 • Current
Market Value: $_____

Fourth Birthday
DC064 • 2 ¾"
Issued: 1995 • Current
Market Value: $_____

Fifth Birthday
DC065 • 2 ¾"
Issued: 1995 • Current
Market Value: $_____

CHERUBS

1

Sixth Birthday
DC066 • 2 ¾"
Issued: 1995 • Current
Market Value: $_____

2

Seventh Birthday
DC067 • 3"
Issued: 1995 • Current
Market Value: $_____

3

Eighth Birthday
DC068 • 3"
Issued: 1995 • Current
Market Value: $_____

4

Ninth Birthday
DC069 • 3"
Issued: 1995 • Current
Market Value: $_____

5

Calendar Collectibles – January
10536 • 4"
Issued: 1998 • Current
Market Value: $_____

6

Calendar Collectibles – February
10537 • 3 ¾"
Issued: 1998 • Current
Market Value: $_____

7

Calendar Collectibles – March
10538 • 4"
Issued: 1998 • Current
Market Value: $_____

8

Calendar Collectibles – April
10539 • 3 ¾"
Issued: 1998 • Current
Market Value: $_____

9

Calendar Collectibles – May
10540 • 3 ½"
Issued: 1998 • Current
Market Value: $_____

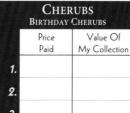

10

Calendar Collectibles – June
10541 • 3 ¾"
Issued: 1998 • Current
Market Value: $_____

CHERUBS
BIRTHDAY CHERUBS

	Price Paid	Value Of My Collection
1.		
2.		
3.		
4.		

CHERUBS
CALENDAR COLLECTIBLES

5.		
6.		
7.		
8.		
9.		
10.		

PENCIL TOTALS

**Calendar Collectibles –
July**
10542 • 3 ¼"
Issued: 1998 • Current
Market Value: $_____

**Calendar Collectibles –
August**
10543 • 3 ½"
Issued: 1998 • Current
Market Value: $_____

**Calendar Collectibles –
September**
10544 • 3 ⅞"
Issued: 1998 • Current
Market Value: $_____

**Calendar Collectibles –
October**
10545 • 3 ¼"
Issued: 1998 • Current
Market Value: $_____

**Calendar Collectibles –
November**
10546 • 3 ⅜"
Issued: 1998 • Current
Market Value: $_____

**Calendar Collectibles –
December**
10547 • 3 ⅜"
Issued: 1998 • Current
Market Value: $_____

CHERUBS
CALENDAR COLLECTIBLES

	Price Paid	Value Of My Collection
1.		
2.		
3.		
4.		
5.		
6.		

CHERUBS
GEMSTONE COLLECTION

7.		
8.		
9.		
10.		

✏ **PENCIL TOTALS**

Garnet (January)
DC434 • 3 ⅝"
Issued: 1997 • Current
Market Value: $_____

Amethyst (February)
DC435 • 3 ½"
Issued: 1997 • Current
Market Value: $_____

Aquamarine (March)
DC436 • 3 ½"
Issued: 1997 • Current
Market Value: $_____

Diamond (April)
DC437 • 3 ¾"
Issued: 1997 • Current
Market Value: $_____

(1)

Emerald (May)
DC438 • 3 ¼"
Issued: 1997 • Current
Market Value: $_____

(2)

Alexandrite (June)
DC439 • 3 ½"
Issued: 1997 • Current
Market Value: $_____

(3)

Ruby (July)
DC440 • 3 ¼"
Issued: 1997 • Current
Market Value: $_____

(4)

Peridot (August)
DC441 • 3 ⅝"
Issued: 1997 • Current
Market Value: $_____

(5)

Sapphire (September)
DC442 • 3 ¾"
Issued: 1997 • Current
Market Value: $_____

(6)

Rose Quartz (October)
DC443 • 3 ½"
Issued: 1997 • Current
Market Value: $_____

(7)

A.

B.
Topaz (November)
DC444 • 3 ¾"
Issued: 1997 • Current
Market Value: A. Yellow Stone – $_____ B. Blue Stone – N/E

(8)

Turquoise (December)
DC445 • 3 ½"
Issued: 1997 • Current
Market Value: $_____

CHERUBS
GEMSTONE COLLECTION

	Price Paid	Value Of My Collection
1.		
2.		
3.		
4.		
5.		
6.		
7.		
8.		

✏ **PENCIL TOTALS**

1 New!

Golden Best Pals
10659 • 4 ¾"
Issued: 1999 • Current
Market Value: $_____

2 New!

Golden Cherub And Child
10656 • 5 ½"
Issued: 1999 • Current
Market Value: $_____

3 New!

Golden Forever Friends
10658 • 4 ½"
Issued: 1999 • Current
Market Value: $_____

4 New!

Golden Heavenly Dreamer
10661 • 5 ½"
Issued: 1999 • Current
Market Value: $____

5 New!

Golden Make A Wish
10663 • 5 ½"
Issued: 1999 • Current
Market Value: $_____

6 New!

Golden Mischief Maker
10660 • 5"
Issued: 1999 • Current
Market Value: $_____

CHERUBS
GOLDEN HALO COLLECTION

	Price Paid	Value Of My Collection
1.		
2.		
3.		
4.		
5.		
6.		
7.		
8.		

PENCIL TOTALS

7 New!

Golden Sitting Pretty
10657 • 3 ¾"
Issued: 1999 • Current
Market Value: $_____

8 New!

Golden Wildflower
10662 • 3 ½"
Issued: 1999 • Current
Market Value: $_____

HOLIDAY CHERUBS

Many of the early Dreamsicles figurines were issued as Holiday Cherubs as well as regular cherubs, each with its own style number. A total of 141 Holiday Cherubs have been released, including 19 Nativity pieces. Holiday Cherubs can be easily recognized by the poinsettias and red berries that decorate their wreaths and by the red ribbons that many of them wear.

1

Away In A Manger
10430 • 6"
Issued: 1998 • Current
Market Value: $_____

2

Baby And Me
DX054 • 3"
Issued: 1994 • Suspended: 1997
Market Value: $18

3

Baby Love
DX147 • 2 ½"
Issued: 1992 • Retired: 1995
Market Value: $20

4

Baby's First Christmas
DX242 • 3"
Issued: 1994 • Suspended: 1997
Market Value: $22

5

Bear Hugs
10436 • 3"
Issued: 1998 • Current
Market Value: $_____

6

Bearing Gifts
DX255 • 2 ½"
Issued: 1996 • Current
Market Value: $_____

7

Bedtime Prayer
DX703 • 3"
Issued: 1995 • Suspended: 1997
Market Value: $15

HOLIDAY CHERUBS

	Price Paid	Value Of My Collection
1.		
2.		
3.		
4.		
5.		
6.		
7.		
✎ PENCIL TOTALS		

HOLIDAY CHERUBS

95

Dreamsicles® — VALUE GUIDE

(1)

Best Buddies
DX159 • 3 ¾"
Issued: 1995 • Suspended: 1996
Market Value: $22

(2)

Best Pals
DX103 • 4 ¾"
Issued: 1991 • Retired: 1994
Market Value: $45

(3)

Birdie And Me
DX056 • 2 ½"
Issued: 1994 • Suspended: 1997
Market Value: $15

(4)

Bluebird On My Shoulder
DX115 • 6"
Issued: 1992 • Retired: 1995
Market Value: $48

(5)

Born This Day
DX230 • 4"
Issued: 1994 • Suspended: 1998
Market Value: $32

(6)

Bright Eyes
DX108 • 3 ½"
Issued: 1991 • Suspended: 1996
Market Value: $18

HOLIDAY CHERUBS

	Price Paid	Value Of My Collection
1.		
2.		
3.		
4.		
5.		
6.		
7.		
8.		
9.		
10.		

✎ PENCIL TOTALS

(7)

Bundle Of Joy
DX142 • 2 ½"
Issued: 1992 • Retired: 1995
Market Value: $20

(8)

Bunny And Me
DX055 • 2 ⅝"
Issued: 1994 • Suspended: 1997
Market Value: $15

(9)

Caroler #1
DX216 • 6 ½"
Issued: 1992 • Retired: 1995
Market Value: $45

(10)

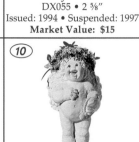

Caroler #2
DX217 • 6 ½"
Issued: 1992 • Retired: 1995
Market Value: $45

(1)

Caroler #3
DX218 • 6 ½"
Issued: 1992 • Retired: 1995
Market Value: $45

(2)

The Carolers
10469 • 3 ¾"
Issued: 1998 • Current
Market Value: $____

(3)

Cherub And Child
DX100 • 5 ½"
Issued: 1991 • Retired: 1995
Market Value: $60

(4)

A Child's Prayer
DX145 • 2 ½"
Issued: 1992 • Retired: 1995
Market Value: $15

(5)

Chimney Cherub
(Early Release – Fall 1998)
10507 • 3 ¾"
Issued: TBA • Current
Market Value: $____

(6)

Christmas Morning
DX710 • 3 ½"
Issued: 1995 • Suspended: 1997
Market Value: N/E

(7)

Christmas Trim
DX711 • 2"
Issued: 1996 • Suspended: 1997
Market Value: $15

(8)

Come Let Us Adore Him
DX475 • 8 ¼"
Issued: 1995 • Suspended: 1997
Market Value: $95

(9)

Deck The Halls
10434 • 2 ¾"
Issued: 1998 • Current
Market Value: $____

(10)

Dream A Little Dream
DX144 • 2 ½"
Issued: 1992 • Retired: 1995
Market Value: $18

HOLIDAY CHERUBS

	Price Paid	Value Of My Collection
1.		
2.		
3.		
4.		
5.		
6.		
7.		
8.		
9.		
10.		
✏ PENCIL TOTALS		

HOLIDAY CHERUBS

Follow Your Star
DX257 • 2 ½"
Issued: 1996 • Suspended: 1998
Market Value: $28

Forever Friends
DX102 • 4 ½"
Issued: 1991 • Retired: 1994
Market Value: $50

Forever Yours
DX110 • 10"
Issued: 1991 • Retired: 1995
Market Value: $85

Forty Winks
DX233 • 3 ½"
Issued: 1995 • Suspended: 1996
Market Value: $25

Free Bird
DX234 • 3 ¾"
Issued: 1995 • Suspended: 1996
Market Value: $20

Gift Wrapped
10437 • 2 ½"
Issued: 1998 • Current
Market Value: $_____

HOLIDAY CHERUBS

	Price Paid	Value Of My Collection
1.		
2.		
3.		
4.		
5.		
6.		
7.		
8.		

✏ PENCIL TOTALS

Gingerbread House
DX254 • 2 ⅝"
Issued: 1996 • Current
Market Value: $_____

Good Shepherd
DX104 • 4"
Issued: 1994 • Suspended: 1997
Market Value: $35

1

Grandma's Or Bust
DX227 • 4"
Issued: 1995 • Suspended: 1996
Market Value: $22

2

Granny's Cookies
DX228 • 2 ½"
Issued: 1995 • Suspended: 1996
Market Value: $18

3

Happy Feet
DX164 • 3"
Issued: 1995 • Suspended: 1996
Market Value: $18

4

Heavenly Dreamer
DX106 • 5 ½"
Issued: 1991 • Retired: 1996
Market Value: $32

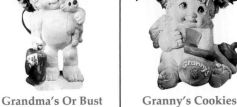

5

Hello Dolly
DX702 • 3 ½"
Issued: 1995 • Suspended: 1997
Market Value: $20

6

Herald Angel
10431 • 3 ¼"
Issued: 1998 • Current
Market Value: $_____

7

Here Comes Trouble
DX214 • 8"
Issued: 1992 • Suspended: 1997
Market Value: N/E

8

Here's Looking At You
DX172 • 4"
Issued: 1994 • Retired: 1995
Market Value: $40

9

Holiday Buddies
10185 • 3 ⅝"
Issued: 1997 • Current
Market Value: $_____

10

Holiday Pals
DX709 • 3 ¾"
Issued: 1995 • Suspended: 1997
Market Value: N/E

HOLIDAY CHERUBS

	Price Paid	Value Of My Collection
1.		
2.		
3.		
4.		
5.		
6.		
7.		
8.		
9.		
10.		

✏ **PENCIL TOTALS**

HOLIDAY CHERUBS

① Hooked On You
(Early Release – Fall 1998)
10623 • 3 ¾"
Issued: TBA • Current
Market Value: $_____

② Hugabye Baby
DX701 • 3"
Issued: 1995 • Retired: 1997
Market Value: $18

③ Hushaby Baby
DX303 • 3 ¾"
Issued: 1995 • Suspended: 1996
Market Value: $22

④ I Love Mommy
DX226 • 2 ¾"
Issued: 1995 • Suspended: 1996
Market Value: $20

⑤ I Love You
DX225 • 4 ½"
Issued: 1995 • Suspended: 1996
Market Value: N/E

⑥ Jingle Bell Rock
(Early Release – Fall 1998)
10615 • 4 ½"
Issued: TBA • Current
Market Value: $_____

HOLIDAY CHERUBS

	Price Paid	Value Of My Collection
1.		
2.		
3.		
4.		
5.		
6.		
7.		
8.		
9.		
10.		

✏ **PENCIL TOTALS**

⑦ Joy Ride
10429 • 3 ¾"
Issued: 1998 • Current
Market Value: $_____

⑧ Joyful Gathering
DX231 • 5"
Issued: 1994 • Suspended: 1998
Market Value: N/E

⑨ Kitty And Me
DX051 • 3"
Issued: 1994 • Suspended: 1997
Market Value: $15

⑩ Let's Play Fetch
DX237 • 4 ½"
Issued: 1995 • Suspended: 1996
Market Value: $22

1	2	3

Life Is Good DX119 • 5 ¼" Issued: 1992 • Retired: 1996 **Market Value: $32**	**Little Darlin'** DX146 • 2 ½" Issued: 1992 • Retired: 1995 **Market Value: $20**	**Littlest Angel** DX143 • 2 ½" Issued: 1992 • Retired: 1995 **Market Value: $25**

4	5	6

Love My Kitty DX130 • 3 ¾" Issued: 1993 • Retired: 1996 **Market Value: $30**	**Love My Puppy** DX131 • 3 ¾" Issued: 1993 • Retired: 1996 **Market Value: $30**	**Love My Teddy** DX132 • 4" Issued: 1993 • Retired: 1996 **Market Value: $30**

7	8

Make A Wish DX118 • 5 ½" Issued: 1992 • Suspended: 1996 **Market Value: $19**	**Makin' A List #2** 10465 • 5 ¼" Issued: 1998 • Current **Market Value: $_____**

9	10
Color Change 	
Mall Santa DX258 • 6" Issued: 1996 • Retired: 1998 **Market Value: $40**	**Me And My Shadow** DX116 • 5 ½" Issued: 1993 • Retired: 1996 **Market Value: $35**

HOLIDAY CHERUBS

	Price Paid	Value Of My Collection
1.		
2.		
3.		
4.		
5.		
6.		
7.		
8.		
9.		
10.		

✎ PENCIL TOTALS

HOLIDAY CHERUBS

Mischief Maker
DX105 • 5"
Issued: 1991 • Retired: 1996
Market Value: $35

Miss Morningstar
DX141 • 7 ¼"
Issued: 1993 • Retired: 1996
Market Value: $50

Moon Dance
DX210 • 5 ½"
Issued: 1995 • Retired: 1996
Market Value: $45

Moonglow
DX235 • 3 ¾"
Issued: 1995 • Suspended: 1996
Market Value: $18

Musical Rest
10432 • 2 ⅜"
Issued: 1998 • Current
Market Value: $_____

My Prayer
DX121 • 5 ½"
Issued: 1992 • Suspended: 1996
Market Value: N/E

HOLIDAY CHERUBS

	Price Paid	Value Of My Collection
1.		
2.		
3.		
4.		
5.		
6.		
7.		
8.		
9.		

✎ **PENCIL TOTALS**

Newborn Cherub
DX168 • 3" wide
Issued: 1994 • Suspended: 1996
Market Value: $25

'Nite 'Nite
DX238 • 4 ½"
Issued: 1995 • Suspended: 1996
Market Value: $22

Noel
DX712 • 2 ⅜"
Issued: 1996 • Suspended: 1997
Market Value: $12

1

North Pole Cherub
(Early Release – Fall 1998)
10467 • 4 ⅜"
Issued: TBA • Current
Market Value: $_____

2

Nursery Rhyme
DX229 • 7"
Issued: 1995 • Suspended: 1995
Market Value: $70

3

Oh Little Star
DX713 • 2 ¼"
Issued: 1996 • Suspended: 1997
Market Value: $12

4

Open Me First
DX243 • 3 ¼"
Issued: 1994 • Suspended: 1997
Market Value: $35

5

Over The Rainbow
DX209 • 6"
Issued: 1995 • Suspended: 1996
Market Value: N/E

6

Poetry In Motion
(Special Edition)
DX113 • 5"
Issued: 1995 • Retired: 1997
Market Value: $120

7

Puppy And Me
DX052 • 3"
Issued: 1994 • Suspended: 1997
Market Value: $15

8

Purr-fect Pals
DX239 • 4 ½"
Issued: 1995 • Suspended: 1996
Market Value: $22

9

Rainbow Rider
DX236 • 4"
Issued: 1995 • Suspended: 1996
Market Value: $22

10

Range Rider
DX305 • 4"
Issued: 1995 • Suspended: 1996
Market Value: $22

HOLIDAY CHERUBS

	Price Paid	Value Of My Collection
1.		
2.		
3.		
4.		
5.		
6.		
7.		
8.		
9.		
10.		

✎ **PENCIL TOTALS**

HOLIDAY CHERUBS

1 Color Change

Read Me A Story
DX123 • 2 ¾"
Issued: 1995 • Suspended: 1996
Market Value: $18

2

Santa Baby
DX256 • 2 ¼"
Issued: 1996 • Current
Market Value: $____

3

Santa's Little Helper
DX109 • 4"
Issued: 1991 • Retired: 1997
Market Value: $15

4

Santa's Shop
10186 • 4 ½"
Issued: 1997 • Suspended: 1998
Market Value: N/E

5

Season Of Joy
10427 • 2 ½"
Issued: 1998 • Current
Market Value: $____

6

Season Of Love
10425 • 3 ¼"
Issued: 1998 • Current
Market Value: $____

HOLIDAY CHERUBS

	Price Paid	Value Of My Collection
1.		
2.		
3.		
4.		
5.		
6.		
7.		
8.		
9.		
10.		

✏ **PENCIL TOTALS**

7

Season Of Peace
10426 • 2 ¾"
Issued: 1998 • Current
Market Value: $____

8

Share The Fun
DX178 • 3 ½"
Issued: 1994 • Suspended: 1996
Market Value: $25

9

Side By Side
DX169 • 4 ¾"
Issued: 1994 • Retired: 1995
Market Value: $60

10

Sing Noel
10438 • 3"
Issued: 1998 • Current
Market Value: $____

(1)

Sitting Pretty
DX101 • 3 ¾"
Issued: 1991 • Retired: 1996
Market Value: $25

(2)

Sleigh Ride
DX122 • 5"
Issued: 1992 • Suspended: 1997
Market Value: $50

(3)

Small Cherub With Hanging Ribbon
5104C • 4 ½"
Issued: 1991 • Suspended: 1992
Market Value: $90

(4)

Snow Ball
10470 • 6 ¼"
Issued: 1998 • Current
Market Value: $_____

(5)

Snow Ride
10468 • 4 ½"
Issued: 1998 • Current
Market Value: $_____

(6)

**Snowbound
(Early Release – Fall 1997)**
10120 • 4 ½"
Issued: TBA • Current
Market Value: $_____

(7)

Snowflake
DX117 • 3 ¼"
Issued: 1994 • Current
Market Value: $_____

(8)

Starlight, Starbright
DX708 • 2"
Issued: 1995 • Suspended: 1997
Market Value: $15

(9)

Stocking Stuffer
10435 • 2 ⅞"
Issued: 1998 • Current
Market Value: $_____

(10)

Stolen Kiss
DX162 • 2 ¼"
Issued: 1994 • Suspended: 1996
Market Value: $20

HOLIDAY CHERUBS

	Price Paid	Value Of My Collection
1.		
2.		
3.		
4.		
5.		
6.		
7.		
8.		
9.		
10.		
✎ PENCIL TOTALS		

HOLIDAY CHERUBS

~~Dreamsicles~~ — Value Guide

①
Super Star
DX704 • 6"
Issued: 1995 • Suspended: 1997
Market Value: N/E

②
Swan Lake
DX163 • 3 ½"
Issued: 1995 • Suspended: 1996
Market Value: $20

③
Sweet Dreams
DX125 • 11"
Issued: 1993 • Retired: 1995
Market Value: $55

④
Sweet Stuff
10433 • 2 ½"
Issued: 1998 • Current
Market Value: $_____

⑤
Swing On A Star
DX208 • 5 ½"
Issued: 1995 • Suspended: 1996
Market Value: $40

⑥
Teacher's Pet
DX124 • 5"
Issued: 1993 • Retired: 1997
Market Value: $35

HOLIDAY CHERUBS

	Price Paid	Value Of My Collection
1.		
2.		
3.		
4.		
5.		
6.		
7.		
8.		
9.		
10.		

✏ **PENCIL TOTALS**

⑦
Teddy And Me
DX053 • 3"
Issued: 1994 • Suspended: 1997
Market Value: $20

⑧
Thinking Of You
DX129 • 9"
Issued: 1993 • Retired: 1997
Market Value: $70

⑨
Three Amigos
DX179 • 3 ¼"
Issued: 1994 • Suspended: 1996
Market Value: $20

⑩
Toyland
(Early Release – Fall 1997)
10255 • 3 ⅞"
Issued: 1998 • Current
Market Value: $_____

Twinkle, Twinkle
DX700 • 3 ½"
Issued: 1995 • Retired: 1997
Market Value: $22

Under The Mistletoe
DX253 • 4 ⅛"
Issued: 1996 • Suspended: 1998
Market Value: $22

Visions Of Sugarplums
DX300 • 5 ½"
Issued: 1996 • Suspended: 1998
Market Value: $45

Wildflower
DX107 • 3 ½"
Issued: 1991 • Retired: 1996
Market Value: $25

Wishin' On A Star
DX120 • 4 ¼"
Issued: 1993 • Suspended: 1996
Market Value: $20

Wistful Thinking
DX707 • 2"
Issued: 1995 • Suspended: 1997
Market Value: $20

You've Got A Friend
DX170 • 6"
Issued: 1994 • Suspended: 1996
Market Value: $45

HOLIDAY CHERUBS

	Price Paid	Value Of My Collection
1.		
2.		
3.		
4.		
5.		
6.		
7.		

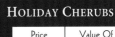
✏ PENCIL TOTALS

HOLIDAY CHERUBS

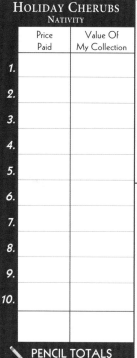

1 Baby Jesus
DX488 • 2 ½"
Issued: 1995 • Current
Market Value: $_____

2 Balthazar
DX481 • 3"
Issued: 1995 • Current
Market Value: $_____

3 Bethlehem Inn
DX474 • 9 ½"
Issued: 1996 • Current
Market Value: $_____

4 Camel
DX477 • 4"
Issued: 1995 • Current
Market Value: $_____

5 Cow
DX480 • 4 ¾"
Issued: 1995 • Current
Market Value: $_____

6 Donkey
DX478 • 3 ¾"
Issued: 1995 • Current
Market Value: $_____

HOLIDAY CHERUBS
NATIVITY

	Price Paid	Value Of My Collection
1.		
2.		
3.		
4.		
5.		
6.		
7.		
8.		
9.		
10.		

✏ PENCIL TOTALS

7 Elephant
DX476 • 4"
Issued: 1995 • Current
Market Value: $_____

8 Gaspar
DX483 • 3 ⅛"
Issued: 1995 • Current
Market Value: $_____

9 Girl With Goose
10477 • 3 ½"
Issued: 1998 • Current
Market Value: $_____

10 Horse
DX479 • 4"
Issued: 1995 • Current
Market Value: $_____

(1)

Joseph
DX485 • 3 ½"
Issued: 1995 • Current
Market Value: $_____

(2)

Little Drummer Boy
10479 • 2 ⅞"
Issued: 1998 • Current
Market Value: $_____

(3)

Mary
DX484 • 2 ⅞"
Issued: 1995 • Current
Market Value: $_____

(4)

Melchior
DX482 • 3 ½"
Issued: 1995 • Current
Market Value: $_____

(5)

Shepherd And Sheep
DX486 • 3 ¾"
Issued: 1995 • Current
Market Value: $_____

(6)

Shepherd With Staff
10478 • 3 ⅞"
Issued: 1998 • Current
Market Value: $_____

(7)

Three Lambs (set/3)
DX487 • 2"
Issued: 1995 • Current
Market Value: $_____

(8)

Miniature Nativity Assortment (set/7)
10489 • Various
Issued: 1998 • Current
Market Value: $_____

(9)

Nativity Collection (set/15)
DX489 • Various
Issued: 1995 • Current
Market Value: $_____

HOLIDAY CHERUBS
NATIVITY

	Price Paid	Value Of My Collection
1.		
2.		
3.		
4.		
5.		
6.		
7.		
8.		
9.		

✏ **PENCIL TOTALS**

Dreamsicles — VALUE GUIDE

HEAVENLY CLASSICS

Originally introduced in 1995, the Heavenly Classics collection consists of 27 pieces. All of the figurines in this group have been either suspended from production or retired. Most of the Heavenly Classics figurines depict Dreamsicles cherubs or children busy at work or play with traditional angel counterparts designed by Cast Art artists Steve and Gigi Hackett.

1

All God's Creatures
HC357 • 7 ¼"
Issued: 1995 • Suspended: 1997
Market Value: $75

2

Bundles Of Love
HC370 • 8"
Issued: 1996 • Suspended: 1996
Market Value: $1,500

3

Crowning Glory
HC359 • 7"
Issued: 1996 • Suspended: 1997
Market Value: $65

HEAVENLY CLASSICS

	Price Paid	Value Of My Collection
1.		
2.		
3.		
4.		
5.		
6.		
7.		

✏ **PENCIL TOTALS**

4

Devoted Companions
HC365 • 4 ½"
Issued: 1996 • Suspended: 1997
Market Value: $30

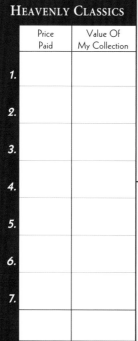

5

Dreamboat
10060 • 7"
Issued: 1997 • Retired: 1997
Market Value: $120

6

First Flight
HC369 • 9 ½"
Issued: 1996 • Suspended: 1997
Market Value: $105

7

Footsteps
HC367 • 5"
Issued: 1996 • Suspended: 1997
Market Value: $30

(1) Color Change

A Gift Of Love
HC366 • 4 ½"
Issued: 1996 • Suspended: 1997
Market Value: $30

(2)

God Bless The Child
HC352 (DC352) • 10"
Issued: 1995 • Suspended: 1997
Market Value: $85

(3)

Heartwarming
HC360 • 6 ½"
Issued: 1996 • Suspended: 1997
Market Value: $85

(4)

Higher Learning
HC353 (DC353) • 6 ½"
Issued: 1995 • Suspended: 1997
Market Value: $100

(5)

Hush Little Baby
HC361 • 7 ¼"
Issued: 1996 • Suspended: 1997
Market Value: $55

(6)

Making Memories
HC381 • 11"
Issued: 1996 • Suspended: 1996
Market Value: $120

(7)

Making Memories
10096 • 11"
Issued: 1997 • Suspended: 1997
Market Value: $100

(8)

Music Appreciation
HC354 (DC354) • 5 ½"
Issued: 1995 • Suspended: 1997
Market Value: $100

(9)

Nature's Blessing
HC364 • 3 ¾"
Issued: 1996 • Suspended: 1997
Market Value: $50

(10)

New Beginnings
10251 • 6 ¼"
Issued: 1997 • Suspended: 1998
Market Value: $45

HEAVENLY CLASSICS

	Price Paid	Value Of My Collection
1.		
2.		
3.		
4.		
5.		
6.		
7.		
8.		
9.		
10.		

✎ PENCIL TOTALS

HEAVENLY CLASSICS

Dreamsicles® — Value Guide

1

Ode To Joy
HC362 • 6 ¾"
Issued: 1996 • Suspended: 1997
Market Value: $60

2

On Wings Of Love
HC355 (DC355) • 9 ½"
Issued: 1995 • Suspended: 1997
Market Value: $110

3

Our Father
HC356 • 4 ¾"
Issued: 1995 • Suspended: 1997
Market Value: $45

4

Power Of Love
HC363 • 6"
Issued: 1996 • Suspended: 1997
Market Value: $50

5

Reach For The Stars
HC382 • 7"
Issued: 1996 • Suspended: 1996
Market Value: $85

6

Reverence
HC350 (DC350) • 7 ½"
Issued: 1995 • Suspended: 1997
Market Value: $125

HEAVENLY CLASSICS

	Price Paid	Value Of My Collection
1.		
2.		
3.		
4.		
5.		
6.		
7.		
8.		
9.		
10.		

✏ PENCIL TOTALS

7

Sleep Little Angel
HC368 • 5 ¾"
Issued: 1996 • Suspended: 1997
Market Value: $70

8

Sounds Of Heaven
10250 • 7 ¼"
Issued: 1997 • Suspended: 1998
Market Value: $45

9

Starry Starry Night
HC358 • 8 ½"
Issued: 1995 • Suspended: 1997
Market Value: $80

10

Winter's Kiss
HC383 • 4 ¾"
Issued: 1996 • Suspended: 1996
Market Value: $45

DREAMSICLES KIDS

Dreamsicles Kids made their debut in 1996 and in the line's first two years of production, over 50 figurines were introduced. The children wear the same sweet faces as the cherubs and often appear with animals in daily scenes that reflect a child's innocent perspective of life. The Dreamsicles Kids collection now consists of 60 figurines, 12 of which are still available.

---

1 Color Change

All I Want
DK040 • 3 ⅜"
Issued: 1996 • Suspended: 1997
Market Value: N/E

2

**Anticipation
(I.C.E. Figurine)**
SP002 • 4 ¼"
Issued: 1997 • Current
Market Value: $_____

3

Apple Dumpling
10059 • 3 ⅞"
Issued: 1997 • Suspended: 1998
Market Value: N/E

4

Apple Polisher
10058 • 4 ⅛"
Issued: 1997 • Suspended: 1998
Market Value: N/E

5

Arctic Pals
10178 • 2 ¾"
Issued: 1997 • Suspended: 1998
Market Value: N/E

6

Baby Bunny
10065 • 4"
Issued: 1997 • Current
Market Value: $_____

7 Color Change

Bear Back Rider
DK025 • 4 ½"
Issued: 1996 • Suspended: 1997
Market Value: N/E

DREAMSICLES KIDS

	Price Paid	Value Of My Collection
1.		
2.		
3.		
4.		
5.		
6.		
7.		
✎ PENCIL TOTALS		

(1)

Beggars' Night
10204 • 4 ¼"
Issued: 1997 • Current
Market Value: $_____

(2)

Bewitched
10601 • 5 ¼"
Issued: 1998 • Current
Market Value: $_____

(3)

By The Sea
10055 • 3 ½"
Issued: 1997 • Suspended: 1998
Market Value: N/E

(4)

Child's Play
DK018 • 2 ⅞"
Issued: 1996 • Suspended: 1998
Market Value: N/E

(5)

Coconut Kids
10008 • 3"
Issued: 1996 • Suspended: 1997
Market Value: N/E

(6)

Color Change

Come All Ye Faithful
DK033 • 3 ¾"
Issued: 1996 • Suspended: 1997
Market Value: N/E

DREAMSICLES KIDS

	Price Paid	Value Of My Collection
1.		
2.		
3.		
4.		
5.		
6.		
7.		
8.		
9.		
10.		

✏ **PENCIL TOTALS**

(7)

Dances With Bears
DK036 • 3 ⅝"
Issued: 1996 • Suspended: 1997
Market Value: N/E

(8)

Diaper Dandy
DK017 • 2 ¾"
Issued: 1996 • Suspended: 1997
Market Value: N/E

(9)

Dream Team
10090 • 3"
Issued: 1997 • Current
Market Value: $_____

(10)

Dreamsicles Kids Logo
DK001 • 4 ¼"
Issued: 1996 • Suspended: 1997
Market Value: N/E

1

Egg-citement
10066 • 4 ⅛"
Issued: 1997 • Current
Market Value: $_____

2

Favorite Toy
10188 • 4 ½"
Issued: 1997 • Suspended: 1998
Market Value: N/E

3 Color Change

The First Noel
DK032 • 3 ½"
Issued: 1996 • Suspended: 1997
Market Value: N/E

4

For My Valentine
DK010 • 3 ⅜"
Issued: 1996 • Suspended: 1997
Market Value: N/E

5

Free Kittens
DK038 • 2 ⅞"
Issued: 1996 • Retired: 1998
Market Value: N/E

6

Free Puppies
DK039 • 2 ¾"
Issued: 1996 • Retired: 1998
Market Value: N/E

7

Frosty Friends
10179 • 2 ½"
Issued: 1997 • Suspended: 1998
Market Value: N/E

8 Color Change

Here's My List
DK022 • 3 ½"
Issued: 1996 • Suspended: 1997
Market Value: N/E

9 Color Change

High Chair High Jinks
DK030 • 3 ⅜"
Issued: 1996 • Suspended: 1997
Market Value: N/E

10

Honey Bunny
DK016 • 2 ¼"
Issued: 1996 • Current
Market Value: $_____

DREAMSICLES KIDS

	Price Paid	Value Of My Collection
1.		
2.		
3.		
4.		
5.		
6.		
7.		
8.		
9.		
10.		
✏ PENCIL TOTALS		

DREAMSICLES KIDS

Dreamsicles® — VALUE GUIDE

① Hug A Bunny

DK015 • 4"
Issued: 1996 • Suspended: 1997
Market Value: N/E

② Hula Honeys

10011 • 3 ½"
Issued: 1996 • Suspended: 1997
Market Value: N/E

③ Joy To The World
Color Change

DK031 • 4"
Issued: 1996 • Suspended: 1997
Market Value: N/E

④ Junior Nurse
Color Change

DK029 • 3"
Issued: 1996 • Current
Market Value: $_____

⑤ Kissing Booth

DK042 • 3 ⅜"
Issued: 1997 • Suspended: 1998
Market Value: N/E

⑥ Light The Candles
Color Change

DK026 • 2 ¾"
Issued: 1996 • Suspended: 1997
Market Value: N/E

DREAMSICLES KIDS

	Price Paid	Value Of My Collection
1.		
2.		
3.		
4.		
5.		
6.		
7.		
8.		
9.		
10.		

✎ PENCIL TOTALS

⑦ Lion's Share

DA663 • 4 ¼"
Issued: 1996 • Current
Market Value: $_____

⑧ Love You, Mom

DK011 • 3 ¾"
Issued: 1996 • Suspended: 1998
Market Value: N/E

⑨ Mama's Girl

DK019 • 2 ¾"
Issued: 1996 • Suspended: 1997
Market Value: N/E

⑩ Mush You Huskies

10180 • 12"
Issued: 1997 • Suspended: 1998
Market Value: N/E

1

My A-B-C's
DK012 • 3"
Issued: 1996 • Suspended: 1997
Market Value: N/E

2

Nutcracker Sweet
10189 • 3 ¼"
Issued: 1997 • Suspended: 1998
Market Value: N/E

3

Ocean Friends
10010 • 5 ½"
Issued: 1996 • Suspended: 1997
Market Value: N/E

4

Piggy Bank
DK024 • 3"
Issued: 1996 • Suspended: 1997
Market Value: N/E

5 Color Change

Please, Santa
DK023 • 3 ½"
Issued: 1996 • Suspended: 1997
Market Value: N/E

6

Pop Goes The Weasel
DK014 • 2 ½"
Issued: 1996 • Suspended: 1997
Market Value: N/E

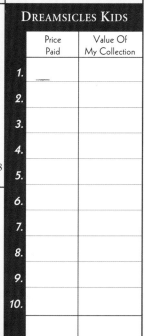

7

Potty Break
10056 • 3"
Issued: 1997 • Suspended: 1998
Market Value: N/E

8

Potty Time
10057 • 3"
Issued: 1997 • Suspended: 1998
Market Value: N/E

9

Pull Toy
DK027 • 4 ¼"
Issued: 1996 • Retired: 1998
Market Value: N/E

10

Punkin
10203 • 4 ½"
Issued: 1997 • Current
Market Value: $_____

DREAMSICLES KIDS

	Price Paid	Value Of My Collection
1.		
2.		
3.		
4.		
5.		
6.		
7.		
8.		
9.		
10.		

✏ PENCIL TOTALS

DREAMSICLES KIDS

1

Rhyme Time
DK013 • 2 ¾"
Issued: 1996 • Suspended: 1997
Market Value: N/E

2

Sand, Sun And Fun
10054 • 2 ⅞"
Issued: 1997 • Suspended: 1998
Market Value: N/E

3 Color Change

Silent Night
DK034 • 3 ⅜"
Issued: 1996 • Suspended: 1997
Market Value: N/E

4 Color Change

Snowball Fight
DK037 • 3 ⅝"
Issued: 1996 • Suspended: 1997
Market Value: N/E

5

Spilt Milk
10053 • 4 ¼"
Issued: 1997 • Suspended: 1997
Market Value: N/E

6

Sunken Treasure
10009 • 3 ½"
Issued: 1996 • Suspended: 1997
Market Value: N/E

DREAMSICLES KIDS

	Price Paid	Value Of My Collection
1.		
2.		
3.		
4.		
5.		
6.		
7.		
8.		
9.		
10.		

✏ **PENCIL TOTALS**

7

Surf's Up
10007 • 3 ½"
Issued: 1996 • Suspended: 1997
Market Value: N/E

8

Three Bears
DK035 • 2 ½"
Issued: 1996 • Suspended: 1997
Market Value: N/E

9

Three Musketeers
DA664 • 4"
Issued: 1996 • Current
Market Value: $_____

10

Toddlin' Tyke
DK020 • 3"
Issued: 1996 • Suspended: 1998
Market Value: N/E

1 Color Change

Visit With Santa
DK021 • 3 ¾"
Issued: 1996 • Suspended: 1997
Market Value: N/E

2

Witchcraft
10602 • 6 ½"
Issued: 1998 • Current
Market Value: $_____

3 Color Change

Young Pups
DK028 • 3 ¼"
Issued: 1996 • Suspended: 1997
Market Value: N/E

DREAMSICLES ANIMALS & OTHER FIGURINES

The 19 animals introduced in 1991 has now grown to a menagerie of several categories of animals and other creatures, which are listed in the Value Guide in the following order: Bears, Birds, Bunnies, Cats, Cows, Dogs, Elephants, Fish, Ghosts & Goblins, Lambs & Sheep, Mice, Musicians, Pigs, Santas & Elves, Witches and Other Figurines. Of the 170 pieces produced, 37 are still current.

4

Beary Sweet
DA455 • 5"
Issued: 1994 • Suspended: 1996
Market Value: $30

5 Original **29**

Buddy Bear
DA451 (5051) • 2 ½"
Issued: 1991 • Retired: 1994
Market Value: $18

6

Clara Bear
DA454 • 5 ½"
Issued: 1995 • Suspended: 1996
Market Value: $24

7

Country Bear
DA458 • 5"
Issued: 1993 • Suspended: 1996
Market Value: $28

DREAMSICLES KIDS

	Price Paid	Value Of My Collection
1.		
2.		
3.		

BEARS

4.		
5.		
6.		
7.		

PENCIL TOTALS

DREAMSICLES KIDS/BEARS

Dreamsicles® — Value Guide

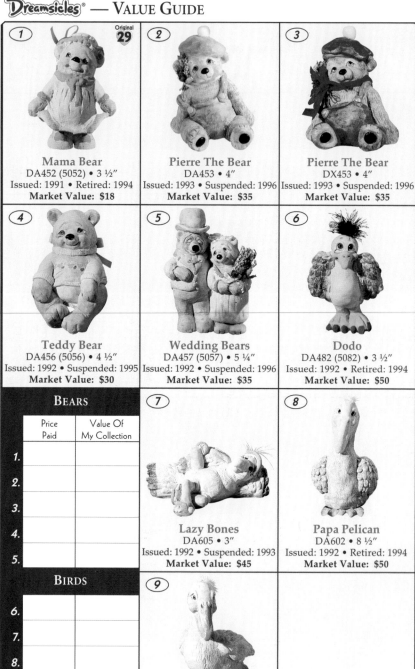

① Original 29

Mama Bear
DA452 (5052) • 3 ½"
Issued: 1991 • Retired: 1994
Market Value: $18

②

Pierre The Bear
DA453 • 4"
Issued: 1993 • Suspended: 1996
Market Value: $35

③

Pierre The Bear
DX453 • 4"
Issued: 1993 • Suspended: 1996
Market Value: $35

④

Teddy Bear
DA456 (5056) • 4 ½"
Issued: 1992 • Suspended: 1995
Market Value: $30

⑤

Wedding Bears
DA457 (5057) • 5 ¼"
Issued: 1992 • Suspended: 1996
Market Value: $35

⑥

Dodo
DA482 (5082) • 3 ½"
Issued: 1992 • Retired: 1994
Market Value: $50

BEARS

	Price Paid	Value Of My Collection
1.		
2.		
3.		
4.		
5.		

BIRDS

6.		
7.		
8.		
9.		

✏ **PENCIL TOTALS**

⑦

Lazy Bones
DA605 • 3"
Issued: 1992 • Suspended: 1993
Market Value: $45

⑧

Papa Pelican
DA602 • 8 ½"
Issued: 1992 • Retired: 1994
Market Value: $50

⑨

Pelican Jr.
DA601 • 5"
Issued: 1992 • Suspended: 1996
Market Value: $42

①
Auntie Bunny
DA120 • 4 ½"
Issued: 1995 • Suspended: 1997
Market Value: $40

②
Bigfoot Bunny
DA121 • 11"
Issued: 1995 • Suspended: 1997
Market Value: $50

③
Binky
10025 • 2"
Issued: 1997 • Current
Market Value: $____

④
Bunny Bouquet
10024 • 6"
Issued: 1997 • Current
Market Value: $____

⑤
Bunny Gardener
DA128 • 4 ¼"
Issued: 1995 • Suspended: 1997
Market Value: N/E

⑥
Original **29**
Bunny Hop
DA105 (5005) • 5 ¼"
Issued: 1991 • Retired: 1995
Market Value: $42

⑦
Bunny Trail
DA125 • 4"
Issued: 1995 • Suspended: 1997
Market Value: N/E

⑧
A Chorus Line
10027 • 2 ⅝"
Issued: 1997 • Current
Market Value: $____

⑨
Colors Of Spring
DA126 • 3 ¼"
Issued: 1995 • Suspended: 1997
Market Value: N/E

⑩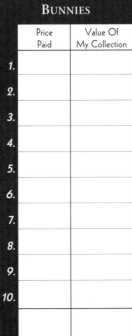
Cupid's Helper
DA203 • 2 ¼"
Issued: 1995 • Current
Market Value: $____

BUNNIES

	Price Paid	Value Of My Collection
1.		
2.		
3.		
4.		
5.		
6.		
7.		
8.		
9.		
10.		

✏ PENCIL TOTALS

BUNNIES

(1)

Dimples
DA100 (5000) • 2 ¼"
Issued: 1991 • Retired: 1995
Market Value: $14

(2)

Easter Surprise
DA115 • 4 ¼"
Issued: 1993 • Suspended: 1997
Market Value: $24

(3)

Egg-citing
DA131 • 2"
Issued: 1995 • Current
Market Value: $_____

(4)

Gathering Flowers
DA320 (5320) • 4 ½"
Issued: 1991 • Retired: 1995
Market Value: $45

(5)

Gathering Flowers
DX320 • 4 ½"
Issued: 1991 • Retired: 1993
Market Value: $45

(6)

Helga
DA112 (5012) • 3 ¼"
Issued: 1992 • Retired: 1995
Market Value: $28

BUNNIES

	Price Paid	Value Of My Collection
1.		
2.		
3.		
4.		
5.		
6.		
7.		
8.		
9.		
10.		

✏ PENCIL TOTALS

(7) Original **29**

Hippity Hop
DA106 (5006) • 9"
Issued: 1991 • Retired: 1994
Market Value: $50

(8)

Hitchin' A Ride
DA321 (5321)• 4 ½"
Issued: 1991 • Suspended: 1997
Market Value: $40

(9) Original **29**

Honey Bun
DA101 (5001) • 2 ¼"
Issued: 1991 • Retired: 1995
Market Value: $18

(10)

Just For You
DA132 • 2"
Issued: 1995 • Current
Market Value: $_____

1

King Rabbit
DA124 (5024) • 18"
Issued: 1991 • Retired: 1994
Market Value: $125

2

Little Sister
DA110 (5010) • 3 ¼"
Issued: 1992 • Suspended: 1997
Market Value: $22

3 Original **29**

Mr. Bunny
DA107 (5007) • 6 ¼"
Issued: 1991 • Retired: 1994
Market Value: $52

4 Original **29**

Mrs. Bunny
DA108 (5008) • 5 ½"
Issued: 1991 • Retired: 1994
Market Value: $52

5

Pal Joey
DA104 • 4 ¾"
Issued: 1993 • Retired: 1995
Market Value: $35

6

Party Bunny
DA116 • 4 ¼"
Issued: 1993 • Suspended: 1995
Market Value: $22

7

Pumpkin Harvest
DA322 (5322) • 4 ½"
Issued: 1991 • Retired: 1994
Market Value: $32

8

St. Peter Rabbit
DA243 • 8"
Issued: 1992 • Retired: 1994
Market Value: $70

9 Original **29**

Santa Bunny
DX203 (5003) • 8 ½"
Issued: 1991 • Retired: 1994
Market Value: $80

10

Sarge
DA111 (5011) • 3 ¼"
Issued: 1992 • Retired: 1995
Market Value: $20

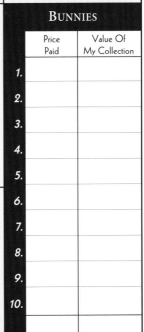

BUNNIES

	Price Paid	Value Of My Collection
1.		
2.		
3.		
4.		
5.		
6.		
7.		
8.		
9.		
10.		

✎ PENCIL TOTALS

BUNNIES

1

Scooter Bunny
DA129 • 2 ½"
Issued: 1995 • Suspended: 1997
Market Value: $14

2

Sir Hareold
DA123 (5023) • 10 ½"
Issued: 1992 • Retired: 1996
Market Value: $75

3

Soap Box Bunny
DA221 (5303) • 4"
Issued: 1991 • Retired: 1995
Market Value: $40

4

Sonny Boy
DA109 (5009) • 3 ¼"
Issued: 1992 • Suspended: 1997
Market Value: $25

5

Steppin' Out
DA130 • 2 ½"
Issued: 1995 • Current
Market Value: $_____

6

Sweetie Pie
10026 • 2 ¼"
Issued: 1997 • Current
Market Value: $_____

BUNNIES

	Price Paid	Value Of My Collection
1.		
2.		
3.		
4.		
5.		
6.		
7.		
8.		
9.		
10.		

PENCIL TOTALS

7

Original **29**

Tiny Bunny
DA102 (5002) • 3"
Issued: 1991 • Retired: 1995
Market Value: $25

8

A Tisket, A Tasket
DA114 • 4 ½"
Issued: 1993 • Suspended: 1997
Market Value: $22

9

Tuckered Out
DA127 • 4 ¾"
Issued: 1995 • Current
Market Value: $_____

10

Uncle Bunny
DA119 • 5"
Issued: 1995 • Suspended: 1997
Market Value: $40

① 	② 	③ 
Cat Nap DA551 (5351) • 5 ½" Issued: 1992 • Suspended: 1995 **Market Value: $20**	**The Cat's Meow** DA552 (5352) • 5" Issued: 1992 • Suspended: 1995 **Market Value: $22**	**Cute As A Button** DA553 (5353) • 4" Issued: 1992 • Suspended: 1995 **Market Value: $28**
④ 	⑤ 	⑥ 
Fat Cat DA555 (5355)• 5 ¼" Issued: 1992 • Retired: 1994 **Market Value: $40**	**Pretty Kitty** DA554 (5354) • 5 ½" Issued: 1992 • Suspended: 1995 **Market Value: $30**	**An Apple A Day** 10531 • 4 ½" Issued: 1998 • Current **Market Value: $_____**

⑦ 	⑧ 
Cafe Au Lait 10533 • 3 ½" Issued: 1998 • Current **Market Value: $_____**	**Carnation** DA379 (5179) • 4" Issued: 1991 • Retired: 1996 **Market Value: $30**
⑨ 	⑩ 
Cow Belle 10532 • 5 ⅜" Issued: 1998 • Current **Market Value: $_____**	**Cowpokes** DA384 • 4 ¾" Issued: 1995 • Suspended: 1997 **Market Value: N/E**

CATS

	Price Paid	Value Of My Collection
1.		
2.		
3.		
4.		
5.		

COWS

6.		
7.		
8.		
9.		
10.		
✏ PENCIL TOTALS		

Cats/Cows

1
Original **29**

Dairy Delight
DA381 (5181) • 5 ½"
Issued: 1991 • Retired: 1995
Market Value: $42

2

Daisy
DA376 • 2 ½"
Issued: 1995 • Suspended: 1997
Market Value: $25

3

Get Along Little Dogie
DA378 (5178) • 3 ½"
Issued: 1991 • Suspended: 1997
Market Value: $22

4

Henrietta
DA383 • 7" wide
Issued: 1994 • Retired: 1996
Market Value: $42

5

Hey Diddle Diddle
DA380 (5180) • 5 ¼"
Issued: 1991 • Retired: 1996
Market Value: $32

6

Moo Cow
DA377 • 4"
Issued: 1993 • Suspended: 1997
Market Value: $20

Cows

	Price Paid	Value Of My Collection
1.		
2.		
3.		
4.		
5.		
6.		
7.		
8.		

Dogs

9.		
10.		

✏ **PENCIL TOTALS**

7

Santa Cow
DX455 • 4 ¾"
Issued: 1995 • Suspended: 1997
Market Value: $32

8
Original **29**

Sweet Cream
DA382 (5182) • 7 ¼"
Issued: 1991 • Retired: 1996
Market Value: $48

9

Hound Dog
DA568 • 3"
Issued: 1992 • Retired: 1994
Market Value: $28

10

Man's Best Friend
DA560 • 3 ½"
Issued: 1992 • Retired: 1994
Market Value: $22

① Puppy Love
DA562 • 3 ½"
Issued: 1992 • Retired: 1994
Market Value: $20

② Red Rover
DA566 • 5 ½"
Issued: 1992 • Retired: 1994
Market Value: $25

③ Scooter
DA567 • 3"
Issued: 1992 • Retired: 1994
Market Value: $28

④ Baby Jumbo
10028 • 3 ⅛"
Issued: 1997 • Suspended: 1998
Market Value: N/E

⑤ Balancing Act
10584 • 4 ⅜"
Issued: 1998 • Current
Market Value: $____

⑥ Bubbles
10585 • 3 ¼"
Issued: 1998 • Current
Market Value: $____

⑦ Center Ring *Color Change*
DA250 • 3"
Issued: 1996 • Suspended: 1998
Market Value: N/E

⑧ Elephant Walk *Color Change*
DA253 • 5 ½"
Issued: 1996 • Suspended: 1998
Market Value: N/E

⑨ Intermission
DA254 • 2 ¼"
Issued: 1996 • Suspended: 1998
Market Value: N/E

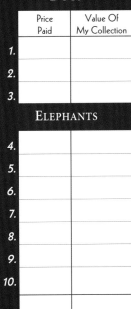

⑩ Peanut Gallery
DA256 • 3 ¼"
Issued: 1996 • Suspended: 1998
Market Value: N/E

DOGS

	Price Paid	Value Of My Collection
1.		
2.		
3.		

ELEPHANTS

4.		
5.		
6.		
7.		
8.		
9.		
10.		

✏ PENCIL TOTALS

DOGS/ELEPHANTS

Dreamsicles® — Value Guide

1

Color Change

Showtime
DA255 • 5"
Issued: 1996 • Suspended: 1998
Market Value: N/E

2

Trunkful Of Love
10029 • 3 ¼"
Issued: 1997 • Suspended: 1998
Market Value: N/E

3

Blowfish
DA608 • 1"
Issued: 1992 • Suspended: 1993
Market Value: $35

4

Double Fish
DA611 • 2 ½"
Issued: 1992 • Suspended: 1993
Market Value: $25

5

Largemouth Bass
DA609 • 3"
Issued: 1992 • Suspended: 1993
Market Value: $25

6

Needlenose Fish
DA610 • 3 ½"
Issued: 1992 • Suspended: 1993
Market Value: $35

ELEPHANTS

	Price Paid	Value Of My Collection
1.		
2.		

FISH

3.		
4.		
5.		
6.		

GHOSTS & GOBLINS

7.		
8.		
9.		
10.		

✏ PENCIL TOTALS

7

Boo!
10587 • 5"
Issued: 1998 • Current
Market Value: $____

8

Boo Babies (set/4)
DA655 • 2"
Issued: 1994 • Current
Market Value: $____

9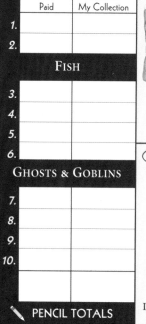

Boo Who?
DA650 (5650) • 4 ½"
Issued: 1991 • Retired: 1996
Market Value: $35

10

Goblins Galore
DA656 • 7 ¼" wide
Issued: 1995 • Current
Market Value: $____

①

Trick Or Treat
DA651 (5651) • 4 ½"
Issued: 1991 • Retired: 1996
Market Value: $40

② Original **29**

Lambie Pie
DA328 (5028) • 4"
Issued: 1991 • Retired: 1994
Market Value: $20

③ Original **29**

Mutton Chops
DA326 (5026) • 2 ½"
Issued: 1991 • Retired: 1994
Market Value: $20

④

Socrates The Sheep
5029 • 5"
Issued: 1991 • Suspended: 1992
Market Value: $95

⑤ Original **29**

Wooley Bully
DA327 (5027) • 2 ¾"
Issued: 1991 • Retired: 1994
Market Value: $25

⑥

Batter Up
10070 • 3"
Issued: 1997 • Suspended: 1997
Market Value: N/E

⑦

Cheesecake
10074 • 2 ¾"
Issued: 1997 • Suspended: 1997
Market Value: N/E

⑧

Color Me Happy
10069 • 3"
Issued: 1997 • Suspended: 1997
Market Value: N/E

⑨

Family Reunion
10072 • 3"
Issued: 1997 • Suspended: 1997
Market Value: N/E

⑩

Fancy Dance
10071 • 3"
Issued: 1997 • Suspended: 1997
Market Value: N/E

GHOSTS & GOBLINS

	Price Paid	Value Of My Collection
1.		

LAMBS & SHEEP

2.		
3.		
4.		
5.		

MICE

6.		
7.		
8.		
9.		
10.		

✏ **PENCIL TOTALS**

GHOSTS/LAMBS/MICE

Dreamsicles® — Value Guide

1

Let It Snow
DA473 • 3"
Issued: 1994 • Suspended: 1997
Market Value: $18

2 Original **29**

Mother Mouse
DA477 (5077) • 4"
Issued: 1991 • Retired: 1994
Market Value: $30

3

Mouse-O'-Lantern
DA472 • 3"
Issued: 1993 • Suspended: 1997
Market Value: $18

4

Mouse On Skis
DA475 (5300) • 4 ½"
Issued: 1991 • Suspended: 1993
Market Value: $40

5 Original **29**

P. J. Mouse
DA476 (5076) • 2 ¾"
Issued: 1991 • Retired: 1994
Market Value: $30

6

Sleigh Bells Ring
DA474 • 2 ¾"
Issued: 1994 • Suspended: 1997
Market Value: $45

MICE

	Price Paid	Value Of My Collection
1.		
2.		
3.		
4.		
5.		
6.		
7.		

MUSICIANS

8.		
9.		
10.		

✏ **PENCIL TOTALS**

7

Sweet On You
10073 • 2 ½"
Issued: 1997 • Suspended: 1997
Market Value: N/E

8

Little Drummer Boy
DX241 • 6"
Issued: 1992 • Suspended: 1996
Market Value: $45

9 Original **29**

Musician With Cymbals
5154 • 7 ¼"
Issued: 1991 • Suspended: 1992
Market Value: $90

10 Original **29**

Musician With Drums
5152 • 8"
Issued: 1991 • Suspended: 1992
Market Value: $100

(1)  Original **29**

Musician With Flute
5153 • 7 ½"
Issued: 1991 • Suspended: 1992
Market Value: $90

(2)  Original **29**

Musician With Trumpet
5151 • 7"
Issued: 1991 • Suspended: 1992
Market Value: $90

(3)

Hambone
DA344 (5044) • 3 ¼"
Issued: 1991 • Retired: 1996
Market Value: $25

(4)

Hamlet
DA342 (5042) • 4 ¼"
Issued: 1991 • Retired: 1996
Market Value: $25

(5)

Kitchen Pig
DA345 (5045) • 8 ½"
Issued: 1991 • Suspended: 1995
Market Value: $65

(6)

Momma Pig
DA347 • 4 ½"
Issued: 1994 • Suspended: 1996
Market Value: $30

(7)

Pappy Pig
DA346 • 4 ¾"
Issued: 1994 • Suspended: 1996
Market Value: $30

(8)

Piglet
DA343 (5043) • 3"
Issued: 1991 • Retired: 1996
Market Value: $28

(9)  Original **29**

Pigmalion
DA340 (5040) • 2"
Issued: 1991 • Retired: 1995
Market Value: $22

(10) Original **29**

Pigtails
DA341 (5041) • 2"
Issued: 1991 • Retired: 1995
Market Value: $22

MUSICIANS

	Price Paid	Value Of My Collection
1.		
2.		

PIGS

3.		
4.		
5.		
6.		
7.		
8.		
9.		
10.		

✏ PENCIL TOTALS

MUSICIANS/PIGS

131

(1)

Pintsize Pigs
DA349 • 3 ½"
Issued: 1994 • Suspended: 1996
Market Value: $35

(2)

Preppie Pig
DA348 • 4 ½"
Issued: 1994 • Suspended: 1996
Market Value: $28

(3) Color Change

Elf Help
DX259 • 3 ¼"
Issued: 1996 • Suspended: 1997
Market Value: N/E

(4)

Father Christmas
DX246 • 8 ½"
Issued: 1993 • Suspended: 1997
Market Value: $60

(5)

Father Christmas #2
10463 • 8"
Issued: 1998 • Current
Market Value: $_____

(6)

Giant Santa
10422 • 14"
Issued: 1998 • Current
Market Value: $_____

PIGS

	Price Paid	Value Of My Collection
1.		
2.		

SANTAS & ELVES

3.		
4.		
5.		
6.		
7.		
8.		
9.		
10.		

PENCIL TOTALS

(7)

Here Comes Santa Claus
DX245 • 18"
Issued: 1991 • Suspended: 1997
Market Value: $90

(8)

Jolly Old Santa
DX244 • 7 ½"
Issued: 1992 • Suspended: 1997
Market Value: $40

(9)

Jolly Old Santa #2
10464 • 7"
Issued: 1998 • Current
Market Value: $_____

(10)

Santa's Elf
DX240 • 5 ½"
Issued: 1991 • Retired: 1996
Market Value: $40

①

Up On The Rooftop
10423 • 5 ¾"
Issued: 1998 • Current
Market Value: $_____

②

Be-Witching
DA652 • 5"
Issued: 1993 • Current
Market Value: $_____

③

Halloween Ride
DA659 • 4"
Issued: 1994 • Current
Market Value: $_____

④

Pumpkin Seed
DA662 • 3"
Issued: 1994 • Current
Market Value: $_____

⑤

Pumpkin Seed
10606 • 3"
Issued: 1998 • Current
Market Value: $_____

⑥

Spellbound
10589 • 6 ⅛"
Issued: 1998 • Current
Market Value: $_____

⑦

Sweeping Beauty
DA661 • 2 ½"
Issued: 1994 • Current
Market Value: $_____

⑧

Sweeping Beauty
10605 • 2 ½"
Issued: 1998 • Current
Market Value: $_____

⑨

Wicked Witch
10592 • 12"
Issued: 1998 • Current
Market Value: $_____

⑩

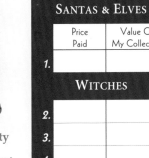

Witch
DA660 (5660) • 5"
Issued: 1991 • Current
Market Value: $_____

	SANTAS & ELVES	
	Price Paid	Value Of My Collection
1.		
	WITCHES	
2.		
3.		
4.		
5.		
6.		
7.		
8.		
9.		
10.		
✏️ **PENCIL TOTALS**		

SANTAS/WITCHES

(1)

Witch's Brew
DA654 • 4"
Issued: 1994 • Current
Market Value: $_____

(2)

Witch's Potion
10588 • 6 ¾"
Issued: 1998 • Current
Market Value: $_____

(3) Original **29**

Armadillo
5176 • 3 ½"
Issued: 1991 • Suspended: 1992
Market Value: $120

(4)

Beach Baby
DA615 • 6 ½"
Issued: 1992 • Retired: 1994
Market Value: $45

(5)

Bundle Up
10473 • 3 ½"
Issued: 1998 • Current
Market Value: $_____

(6)

Crabby
DA607 • 2 ½"
Issued: 1992 • Suspended: 1993
Market Value: $32

WITCHES

	Price Paid	Value Of My Collection
1.		
2.		

OTHER FIGURINES

3.		
4.		
5.		
6.		
7.		
8.		
9.		
10.		

✏ **PENCIL TOTALS**

(7)

Dilly
10599 • 3"
Issued: 1998 • Current
Market Value: $_____

(8)

Dino
DA480 (5080) • 4 ¼"
Issued: 1992 • Retired: 1994
Market Value: $55

(9)

Free Ride
DA631 (5031) • 3 ½"
Issued: 1992 • Suspended: 1996
Market Value: $50

(10)

Happy Sailing
DA220 (5301) • 3 ¾"
Issued: 1991 • Retired: 1994
Market Value: $35

1

Li'l Chick
DA385 • 2"
Issued: 1993 • Suspended: 1995
Market Value: $18

2

Li'l Duck
DA388 • 2"
Issued: 1993 • Suspended: 1995
Market Value: $18

3
New!

Mom's Taxi
10736 • 3 ¾"
Issued: 1999 • Current
Market Value: $_____

4

Naptime
DA556 • 2 ¾"
Issued: 1996 • Suspended: 1996
Market Value: $28

5

Octopus' Garden
DA606 • 4"
Issued: 1992 • Suspended: 1993
Market Value: $45

6
Color Change

Opening Night
DA252 • 4"
Issued: 1996 • Suspended: 1998
Market Value: N/E

7

Prancer
DX202 • 8"
Issued: 1991 • Suspended: 1997
Market Value: $60

8

Rhino
DA481 (5081) • 4"
Issued: 1992 • Retired: 1994
Market Value: $45

9

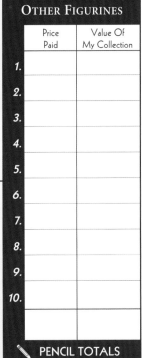

Ricky Raccoon
5170 • 6 ½"
Issued: 1991 • Suspended: 1992
Market Value: $95

10

Scarecrow & Friends
DA653 • 3"
Issued: 1993 • Current
Market Value: $_____

OTHER FIGURINES

	Price Paid	Value Of My Collection
1.		
2.		
3.		
4.		
5.		
6.		
7.		
8.		
9.		
10.		

✎ PENCIL TOTALS

OTHER FIGURINES

1

Sledding
10472 • 4"
Issued: 1998 • Current
Market Value: $_____

2

Slow Poke
DA630 (5030) • 4 ½"
Issued: 1992 • Suspended: 1995
Market Value: $45

3

Snowman
DX252 • 3 ½"
Issued: 1991 • Suspended: 1996
Market Value: $20

4

Splash
DA616 • 6 ¼"
Issued: 1993 • Retired: 1994
Market Value: $60

5

Three On A Sled
DX454 • 4"
Issued: 1994 • Suspended: 1997
Market Value: $35

6

Water Ballet
10006 • 5"
Issued: 1996 • Suspended: 1997
Market Value: N/E

7

Winter's Comin'
DA471 (5171) • 4 ½"
Issued: 1991 • Suspended: 1993
Market Value: $42

OTHER FIGURINES

	Price Paid	Value Of My Collection
1.		
2.		
3.		
4.		
5.		
6.		
7.		

✎ PENCIL TOTALS

ANGEL HUGS

The newest category in the Dreamsicles Collection, "Angel Hugs" are beanbag plush counterparts of Dreamsicles cherubs and animals. Six "Angel Hugs" were issued in early 1999. The first group consists of three cherubs and three winged animals: a bear, a cow and an elephant. "Snowflake," a pure white cherub with a pink heart on its chest, was included in the 1999 Dreamsicles Club kits as an extra benefit (see Dreamsicles Club section on page 37 for details).

---

1 New!

Bluebeary
08002 • 7 ½"
Issued: 1999 • Current
Market Value: $_____

2 New!

Creampuff
08001 • 8 ½"
Issued: 1999 • Current
Market Value: $_____

3 New!

Cupcake
08003 • 8 ½"
Issued: 1999 • Current
Market Value: $_____

4 New!

Daisy
08004 • 5 ½"
Issued: 1999 • Current
Market Value: $_____

5 New!

Peaches
08005 • 8 ½"
Issued: 1999 • Current
Market Value: $_____

6 New!

Peanut
08006 • 5"
Issued: 1999 • Current
Market Value: $_____

ANGEL HUGS

	Price Paid	Value Of My Collection
1.		
2.		
3.		
4.		
5.		
6.		
✎ PENCIL TOTALS		

ANGEL HUGS

OTHER DREAMSICLES COLLECTIBLES

Through the years, Cast Art has offered a variety of Dreamsicles pieces to complement the figurine collection, ranging from bells, boxes and clocks to champagne flutes, candle holders and picture frames. Many of these pieces have wedding or Valentine's Day themes, and of the 229 pieces produced, 140 are still currently available.

1

The Finishing Touches
DS201 • 4 ½"
Issued: 1995 • Retired: 1995
Market Value: $20

2

Santa In Dreamsicle Land
DS216 • 4 ½"
Issued: 1996 • Retired: 1996
Market Value: $20

3

Star Of Wonder
10143 • 4"
Issued: 1997 • Retired: 1997
Market Value: $20

BELLS

	Price Paid	Value Of My Collection
1.		
2.		
3.		

BOOKENDS

4.		
5.		
6.		
7.		

4

Bunny Bookends (pair)
DA122 (5022) • 5 ¼"
Issued: 1992 • Suspended: 1995
Market Value: $90

5

Bunny Bookends (pair)
5021 • 5 ¼"
Issued: 1992 • Suspended: 1992
Market Value: $110

6

Cherub Bookends (pair)
10403 • 6 ½"
Issued: 1998 • Current
Market Value: $_____

7

Cherub Bookends (pair)
10404 • 6 ½"
Issued: 1998 • Current
Market Value: $_____

PENCIL TOTALS

1

Little Dickens
DC127 • 5 ½"
Issued: 1993 • Retired: 1995
Market Value: $45

2

Little Dickens
DX127 • 5 ½"
Issued: 1993 • Retired: 1995
Market Value: $45

3

Long Fellow
DC126 • 5 ½"
Issued: 1993 • Retired: 1995
Market Value: $45

4

Long Fellow
DX126 • 5 ½"
Issued: 1993 • Retired: 1995
Market Value: $45

5

Birdbath Box
10598 • 4 ⅜"
Issued: 1998 • Current
Market Value: $_____

6

Bluebird Box
10035 • 4"
Issued: 1997 • Current
Market Value: $____

7

Cherub In Manger Box
10456 • 4 ⅜"
Issued: 1998 • Current
Market Value: $_____

8

Christmas Ark Box
10457 • 4"
Issued: 1998 • Current
Market Value: $_____

9

Christmas Train Box
10192 • 4 ½"
Issued: 1997 • Current
Market Value: $_____

10

Dear To My Heart Box
10629 • 4"
Issued: 1999 • Current
Market Value: $_____

BOOKENDS

	Price Paid	Value Of My Collection
1.		
2.		
3.		
4.		

BOXES

5.		
6.		
7.		
8.		
9.		
10.		

✏ **PENCIL TOTALS**

BOOKENDS/BOXES

ᴰʳᵉᵃᵐˢⁱᶜˡᵉˢ® — Value Guide

First Christmas Box
10191 • 4 ½"
Issued: 1997 • Current
Market Value: $_____

Flower Cart Box
10353 • 4 ¼"
Issued: 1998 • Current
Market Value: $_____

Guardian Angel Box
10037 • 3 ½"
Issued: 1997 • Current
Market Value: $_____

Here Comes Trouble Box
10190 • 4 ¾"
Issued: 1997 • Current
Market Value: $_____

**King Heart
"I Love You" Box**
5850 • 7 ½"
Issued: 1991 • Suspended: 1992
Market Value: N/E

King Oval Cow Box
5860 • 10 ½"
Issued: 1991 • Suspended: 1992
Market Value: N/E

Boxes

	Price Paid	Value Of My Collection
1.		
2.		
3.		
4.		
5.		
6.		
7.		
8.		
9.		
10.		

✎ **PENCIL TOTALS**

Kiss, Kiss Box
10034 • 4"
Issued: 1997 • Current
Market Value: $_____

**Medium Heart
Cherub Box**
5751 • 4"
Issued: 1991 • Suspended: 1992
Market Value: $140

**Medium Octagonal
Bunny Box**
5752 • 4"
Issued: 1991 • Suspended: 1992
Market Value: N/E

**Medium Square
"Speed Racer" Box**
5750 • 4 ½"
Issued: 1991 • Suspended: 1992
Market Value: N/E

① New!

Morning Glory Birdhouse Box
10769 • 3 ½"
Issued: 1999 • Current
Market Value: $____

②

Octagonal Ballerina Box
5700 • 3"
Issued: 1991 • Suspended: 1992
Market Value: N/E

③ New!

Pansies Birdhouse Box
10770 • 3 ¾"
Issued: 1999 • Current
Market Value: $____

④ New!

Pink Roses Birdhouse Box
10771 • 3 ⅜"
Issued: 1999 • Current
Market Value: $____

⑤

Queen Octagonal Cherub Box
5804 • 6 ½"
Issued: 1991 • Suspended: 1992
Market Value: $140

⑥

Queen Rectangle Cat Box
5800 • 6 ½"
Issued: 1991 • Suspended: 1992
Market Value: N/E

⑦

Queen Rectangle Train Box
5803 • 7"
Issued: 1991 • Suspended: 1992
Market Value: N/E

⑧

Queen Round Bears Box
5801 • 7"
Issued: 1991 • Suspended: 1992
Market Value: N/E

⑨

Queen Square "You're Special" Box
5802 • 6"
Issued: 1991 • Suspended: 1992
Market Value: N/E

⑩

Reindeer Rider Box
10455 • 5"
Issued: 1998 • Current
Market Value: $____

BOXES

	Price Paid	Value Of My Collection
1.		
2.		
3.		
4.		
5.		
6.		
7.		
8.		
9.		
10.		

✏ PENCIL TOTALS

BOXES

1

Santa's Helper Box
10193 • 4 ¼"
Issued: 1997 • Current
Market Value: $_____

2

Small Heart
"I Love You" Box
5701 • 3 ¼"
Issued: 1991 • Suspended: 1992
Market Value: $95

3

Small Rectangle
"Dicky Duck" Box
5703 • 3 ½"
Issued: 1991 • Suspended: 1992
Market Value: $90

4

Small Square
Dinosaur Box
5702 • 3"
Issued: 1991 • Suspended: 1992
Market Value: $140

5 *New!*

Stolen Kiss Box
10630 • 4 ½"
Issued: 1999 • Current
Market Value: $_____

6 *New!*

Sunflower
Birdhouse Box
10772 • 3 ⅝"
Issued: 1999 • Current
Market Value: $_____

BOXES

	Price Paid	Value Of My Collection
1.		
2.		
3.		
4.		
5.		
6.		
7.		
8.		
9.		

✏ PENCIL TOTALS

7

Tiny Dancer Box
10036 • 4 ¼"
Issued: 1997 • Current
Market Value: $_____

8

Watering Can Box
10597 • 4"
Issued: 1998 • Current
Market Value: $_____

9 *New!*

Wedding Cake Box
10758 • 4"
Issued: 1999 • Current
Market Value: $_____

(1)

Flight School
DC340 • 4 ⅜"
Issued: 1996 • Suspended: 1997
Market Value: $70

(2)

Star Factory
DC341 • 4 ⅜"
Issued: 1996 • Suspended: 1997
Market Value: $65

(3)

Wreath Maker
10080 • 4"
Issued: 1997 • Suspended: 1997
Market Value: $60

(4) *New!*

Cake Topper
10757 • 6 ⅜"
Issued: 1999 • Current
Market Value: $____

(5)

All Aglow
10471 • 3 ¾"
Issued: 1998 • Current
Market Value: $____

(6) *New!*

Bride & Groom Candlestick
10759 • 4 ¼"
Issued: 1999 • Current
Market Value: $____

(7)

Cherub Moon
10453 • 3"
Issued: 1998 • Current
Market Value: $____

(8)

Cherub Star
10454 • 3"
Issued: 1998 • Current
Market Value: $____

(9)

Chill Chaser
(Early Release – Fall 1997)
10117 • 4 ½"
Issued: TBA • Current
Market Value: $____

(10)

Dream Street
10118 • 5 ¼"
Issued: 1997 • Current
Market Value: $____

	Price Paid	Value Of My Collection
BUILDINGS		
1.		
2.		
3.		
CAKE TOPPERS		
4.		
CANDLE & VOTIVE HOLDERS		
5.		
6.		
7.		
8.		
9.		
10.		
✏ **PENCIL TOTALS**		

Dreamsicles® — VALUE GUIDE

1

Fireside Fun
DK041 • 3″
Issued: 1996 • Current
Market Value: $_____

2

Good Will To Men
10424 • 9 ¼″ wide
Issued: 1998 • Current
Market Value: $_____

3

Large Candle Holder #1
DC138 • 6″
Issued: 1993 • Retired: 1994
Market Value: $65

4

Large Candle Holder #2
DC139 • 6″
Issued: 1993 • Retired: 1994
Market Value: $65

5

Light My Way
10122 • 3 ¾″
Issued: 1997 • Current
Market Value: $_____

6

Pumpkin Capers
10201 • 3 ½″
Issued: 1997 • Current
Market Value: $_____

CANDLE & VOTIVE HOLDERS

	Price Paid	Value Of My Collection
1.		
2.		
3.		
4.		
5.		
6.		
7.		
8.		
9.		
10.		

✎ PENCIL TOTALS

7

Pumpkin Pretender
10202 • 3 ¼″
Issued: 1997 • Current
Market Value: $_____

8

Small Candle Holder #1
DC136 • 2 ½″
Issued: 1993 • Suspended: 1996
Market Value: $30

9

Small Candle Holder #1
DX136 • 2 ½″
Issued: 1994 • Suspended: 1997
Market Value: $30

10

Small Candle Holder #2
DC137 • 2 ½″
Issued: 1993 • Suspended: 1996
Market Value: $25

1

Small Candle Holder #2
DX137 • 2 ½"
Issued: 1994 • Suspended: 1997
Market Value: $25

2

Star Of Wonder
10145 • 3 ½"
Issued: 1997 • Retired: 1997
Market Value: $20

3

Star Of Wonder
10148 • 3"
Issued: 1997 • Retired: 1997
Market Value: $22

4

Strange Brew
10200 • 4 ¼"
Issued: 1997 • Current
Market Value: $_____

5

**Two Log Night
(Early Release – Fall 1997)**
10119 • 4"
Issued: 1998 • Current
Market Value: $_____

6

Warm Wishes
DC359 • 4"
Issued: 1996 • Current
Market Value: $_____

7

New!

You Light Up My Life
10640 • 3"
Issued: 1999 • Current
Market Value: $_____

8

**The Wedding Toast
(set/2)**
10218 • 8 ⅝"
Issued: 1997 • Current
Market Value: $_____

9

Grandfather Clock
10209 • 5 ¾"
Issued: 1997 • Current
Market Value: $_____

10

Heart Clock
10211 • 3 ¼"
Issued: 1997 • Current
Market Value: $_____

CANDLE & VOTIVE HOLDERS

	Price Paid	Value Of My Collection
1.		
2.		
3.		
4.		
5.		
6.		
7.		

CHAMPAGNE FLUTES

8.		

CLOCKS

9.		
10.		

 PENCIL TOTALS

CANDLE & VOTIVE HOLDERS/
CHAMPAGNE FLUTES/CLOCKS

Dreamsicles® — VALUE GUIDE

①

Kissing Clock
10530 • 3 ⅛"
Issued: 1998 • Current
Market Value: $_____

②

Mantle Clock
10210 • 3 ¾"
Issued: 1997 • Current
Market Value: $_____

③

Wedding Clock
10529 • 3 ½"
Issued: 1998 • Current
Market Value: $_____

④

Cherub & Bear Egg
10459 • 4 ½"
Issued: 1998 • Current
Market Value: $_____

⑤

Cherub Nativity Egg
10458 • 4 ½"
Issued: 1998 • Current
Market Value: $_____

⑥

Heaven's Little Helper Egg
10390 • 4 ½"
Issued: 1998 • Current
Market Value: $_____

CLOCKS

	Price Paid	Value Of My Collection
1.		
2.		
3.		

EGGS

4.		
5.		
6.		
7.		
8.		
9.		
10.		

✏ **PENCIL TOTALS**

⑦

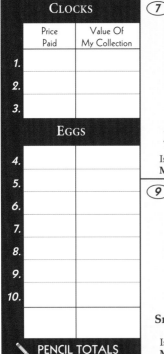

Join The Fun Egg
10394 • 4 ½"
Issued: 1998 • Current
Market Value: $_____

⑧

Merry-Go-Round Egg
10391 • 4 ½"
Issued: 1998 • Current
Market Value: $_____

⑨

Snuggle Blanket Egg
10393 • 4 ½"
Issued: 1998 • Current
Market Value: $_____

⑩

Sweethearts Egg
10392 • 4 ½"
Issued: 1998 • Current
Market Value: $_____

VALUE GUIDE — Dreamsicles®

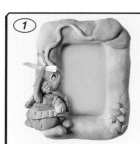

1

Balloons Frame
DF005 • 3 ½"
Issued: 1993 • Suspended: 1994
Market Value: N/E

2

Circus Buddies
10586 • 5 ½"
Issued: 1998 • Current
Market Value: $_____

3

Column Picture Frame
10224 • 7"
Issued: 1997 • Current
Market Value: $_____

New!

4

Double Heart Frame
10641 • 5"
Issued: 1999 • Current
Market Value: $_____

5

Heart Picture Frame
10225 • 4 ½"
Issued: 1997 • Current
Market Value: $_____

6

Kite Frame
DF006 • 3 ½"
Issued: 1993 • Suspended: 1994
Market Value: N/E

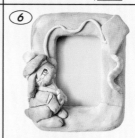

7

Large Heart Frame
DF002 • 4"
Issued: 1993 • Suspended: 1994
Market Value: N/E

8

Oval Frame
DF004 • 3 ⅞"
Issued: 1993 • Suspended: 1994
Market Value: N/E

9

Small Heart Frame
DF001 • 3 ⅜"
Issued: 1993 • Suspended: 1994
Market Value: N/E

10

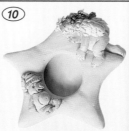

Star Frame
DF003 • 3 ⅛"
Issued: 1993 • Suspended: 1994
Market Value: N/E

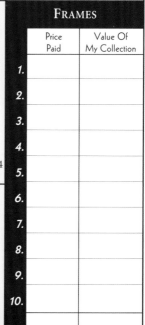

FRAMES

	Price Paid	Value Of My Collection
1.		
2.		
3.		
4.		
5.		
6.		
7.		
8.		
9.		
10.		

✎ PENCIL TOTALS

FRAMES

147

Dreamsicles® — VALUE GUIDE

1

Surrounded By Love Frame
10222 • 6 ¼"
Issued: 1997 • Current
Market Value: $_____

2

New!

Wedding Bells Frame
10760 • 8 ¼"
Issued: 1999 • Current
Market Value: $_____

3

Bigtop Ballet (Early Release – Spring 1998)
♪ *Music Box Dancer*
10207 • 5 ⅛"
Issued: 1998 • Current
Market Value: $_____

4

Birthday Surprise (Early Release – Fall 1997)
♪ *My Favorite Things*
10152 • 5 ⅛"
Issued: 1998 • Current
Market Value: $_____

5

Carousel Ride
♪ *Carousel Waltz*
DS283 • 11 ¼"
Issued: 1996 • Retired: 1998
Market Value: N/E

6

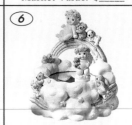

Cherub Twirler
♪ *Music Box Dancer*
10363 • 5 ¾"
Issued: 1998 • Current
Market Value: $_____

FRAMES

	Price Paid	Value Of My Collection
1.		
2.		

MUSICALS & WATERGLOBES

3.		
4.		
5.		
6.		
7.		
8.		
9.		
10.		

✏ PENCIL TOTALS

7

Coming To Town
♪ *Santa Claus Is Coming To Town*
10206 • 6"
Issued: 1997 • Current
Market Value: $_____

8

Dance Ballerina Dance
♪ *Music Box Dancer*
DC140 • 8"
Issued: 1992 • Retired: 1995
Market Value: $90

9

Dance With Me
♪ *Dance of The Sugarplum Fairy*
HC103 • 6"
Issued: 1996 • Suspended: 1997
Market Value: N/E

10

Dreamboat (Early Release – Fall 1997)
♪ *Wind Beneath My Wings*
10154 • 6 ¼"
Issued: TBA • Current
Market Value: $_____

1

Floral Carousel
♪ *Wind Beneath My Wings*
10596 • 11 ¼"
Issued: 1998 • Current
Market Value: $_____

2

Flying High
♪ *Wind Beneath My Wings*
10302 • 7 ¼"
Issued: 1998 • Current
Market Value: $_____

3

The Flying Lesson
♪ *We've Only Just Begun*
DS281 • 5"
Issued: 1996 • Suspended: 1997
Market Value: N/E

4

God Bless The Child
HC107 • 5"
Issued: 1996 • Suspended: 1997
Market Value: N/E

5

Heart To Heart
♪ *Cherish*
HC100 • 6"
Issued: 1996 • Suspended: 1997
Market Value: N/E

6

Hush Little Baby
HC104 • 4 ½"
Issued: 1996 • Suspended: 1997
Market Value: N/E

7

Jumbo Ride
♪ *You Light Up My Life*
10049 • 6 ½"
Issued: 1997 • Suspended: 1997
Market Value: N/E

8

Jump Over The Moon
♪ *Twinkle, Twinkle Little Star*
10377 • 6"
Issued: 1998 • Current
Market Value: $_____

9 *New!*

Lullaby And Goodnight
(Early Release – Fall 1998)
♪ *Brahms' Lullaby*
10613 • 6 ⅝"
Issued: 1999 • Current
Market Value: $_____

10 *New!*

The May Pole
(Early Release – Fall 1998)
♪ *Carousel Waltz*
10614 • 6 ¼"
Issued: 1999 • Current
Market Value: $_____

MUSICALS & WATERGLOBES

	Price Paid	Value Of My Collection
1.		
2.		
3.		
4.		
5.		
6.		
7.		
8.		
9.		
10.		
✎ PENCIL TOTALS		

MUSICALS & WATERGLOBES

① New!

The Melody Makers
(Early Release – Fall 1998)
♪ *We've Only Just Begun*
10611 • 5″
Issued: 1999 • Current
Market Value: $_____

②

Merry-Go-Round
♪ *Memories*
DS278 • 7″
Issued: 1995 • Suspended: 1997
Market Value: N/E

③

Moonstruck
♪ *You've Got A Friend*
DS277 • 7″
Issued: 1995 • Suspended: 1997
Market Value: N/E

④

Music Lesson
♪ *Memories*
HC102 • 6″
Issued: 1996 • Suspended: 1997
Market Value: N/E

⑤

My Special Angel
♪ *Impossible Dream*
HC101 • 5 ½″
Issued: 1996 • Suspended: 1997
Market Value: N/E

⑥

Oh Christmas Tree
♪ *O Tannenbaum*
DS276 • 7 ⅛″
Issued: 1995 • Suspended: 1997
Market Value: N/E

⑦

On Wings Of Love
HC106 • 5″
Issued: 1996 • Suspended: 1997
Market Value: N/E

⑧

Our Father
HC105 • 4 ½″
Issued: 1996 • Suspended: 1997
Market Value: N/E

⑨

Pirouette
♪ *Music Box Dancer*
DS279 • 6 ½″
Issued: 1995 • Suspended: 1997
Market Value: N/E

⑩ New!

Rise And Shine
(Early Release – Fall 1998)
♪ *Over The Rainbow*
10612 • 5 ⅛″
Issued: 1999 • Current
Market Value: $_____

MUSICALS &
WATERGLOBES

	Price Paid	Value Of My Collection
1.		
2.		
3.		
4.		
5.		
6.		
7.		
8.		
9.		
10.		

✎ **PENCIL TOTALS**

1

Shooting Star
♪ *Twinkle, Twinkle Little Star*
DS275 • 6 ⅛"
Issued: 1995 • Suspended: 1997
Market Value: N/E

2

Sleep Tight
(Early Release – Fall 1997)
♪ *Rock-A-Bye Baby*
10153 • 4 ¼"
Issued: 1998 • Current
Market Value: $_____

3

Star Of Wonder
♪ *Silent Night*
10149 • 5 ½"
Issued: 1997 • Current
Market Value: $_____

4

Star Seekers (revolving)
♪ *Somewhere Out There*
HC109 • 6"
Issued: 1996 • Suspended: 1997
Market Value: N/E

5

Starry Starry Night
♪ *Love Story*
HC108 • 5"
Issued: 1996 • Suspended: 1997
Market Value: N/E

6

Stolen Kiss
♪ *Love Story*
DS282 • 5 ¾"
Issued: 1996 • Suspended: 1997
Market Value: N/E

7

Swanderful
♪ *Memories*
10048 • 6 ½"
Issued: 1997 • Suspended: 1997
Market Value: N/E

8

Teeter Tots
♪ *Over The Rainbow*
DS280 • 6"
Issued: 1996 • Suspended: 1997
Market Value: N/E

9

Together Forever
♪ *Endless Love*
10303 • 7"
Issued: 1998 • Current
Market Value: $_____

10

Top Of The World (Early
Release – Spring 1998)
♪ *I'm Sitting On Top Of The World*
10208 • 6"
Issued: TBA • Current
Market Value: $_____

MUSICALS & WATERGLOBES

	Price Paid	Value Of My Collection
1.		
2.		
3.		
4.		
5.		
6.		
7.		
8.		
9.		
10.		

✐ **PENCIL TOTALS**

MUSICALS & WATERGLOBES

(1)

**Two By Two (Early
Release – Spring 1998)**
♪ *Over The Rainbow*
10304 • 6″
Issued: 1998 • Current
Market Value: $_____

(2)

Wedding Vows
♪ *The Wedding March*
10223 • 6″
Issued: 1997 • Current
Market Value: $_____

(3)

Whale Of A Time
♪ *You've Got A Friend*
10047 • 6 ¼″
Issued: 1997 • Suspended: 1997
Market Value: N/E

(4)

Baby's First
10136 • 3″
Issued: 1997 • Current
Market Value: $_____

(5)

Bear
DX274 • 2 ½″
Issued: 1991 • Suspended: 1993
Market Value: $28

(6)

Bunny
DX270 • 2 ½″
Issued: 1991 • Suspended: 1993
Market Value: $28

MUSICALS & WATERGLOBES

	Price Paid	Value Of My Collection
1.		
2.		
3.		

ORNAMENTS

4.		
5.		
6.		
7.		
8.		
9.		
10.		

✏ PENCIL TOTALS

(7)

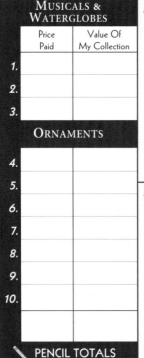

Cherub Facing Bunny
DX283 • 2″
Issued: 1994 • Current
Market Value: $_____

(8)

**Cherub Hands
On Cheeks**
10442 • 5″
Issued: 1998 • Current
Market Value: $_____

(9)

**Cherub Hands
Under Chin**
10440 • 5″
Issued: 1998 • Current
Market Value: $_____

(10)

Cherub On Cloud
DX263 • 2 ½″
Issued: 1991 • Suspended: 1993
Market Value: $28

①

Cherub On Skis
10446 • 2 ¾"
Issued: 1998 • Current
Market Value: $_____

②

Cherub On Sled
10449 • 2"
Issued: 1998 • Current
Market Value: $_____

③

Cherub On Train
10447 • 3"
Issued: 1998 • Current
Market Value: $_____

④

Cherub With Baby
DX286 • 2"
Issued: 1994 • Current
Market Value: $_____

⑤

Cherub With Bear
DX282 • 2"
Issued: 1994 • Current
Market Value: $_____

⑥

Cherub With Bell
10448 • 2 ¾"
Issued: 1998 • Current
Market Value: $_____

⑦

Cherub With Bird
DX287 • 2"
Issued: 1994 • Current
Market Value: $_____

⑧

Cherub With Book
DX280 • 2"
Issued: 1994 • Current
Market Value: $_____

⑨

Cherub With Bunny
DX288 • 2"
Issued: 1994 • Current
Market Value: $_____

⑩

Cherub With Drum
DX281 • 2"
Issued: 1994 • Current
Market Value: $_____

ORNAMENTS

	Price Paid	Value Of My Collection
1.		
2.		
3.		
4.		
5.		
6.		
7.		
8.		
9.		
10.		

✏ PENCIL TOTALS

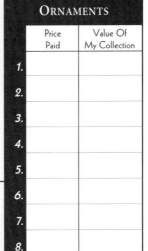

ORNAMENTS

Cherub With Flute
DX285 • 2"
Issued: 1994 • Current
Market Value: $_____

Cherub With Horn
DX289 • 2"
Issued: 1994 • Current
Market Value: $_____

Cherub With Lamb
10450 • 2 ⅜"
Issued: 1998 • Current
Market Value: $_____

Cherub With Lute
10444 • 5"
Issued: 1998 • Current
Market Value: $_____

Cherub With Moon
DX260 • 2 ½"
Issued: 1991 • Suspended: 1993
Market Value: $28

Cherub With Reindeer
10451 • 3"
Issued: 1998 • Current
Market Value: $_____

ORNAMENTS

	Price Paid	Value Of My Collection
1.		
2.		
3.		
4.		
5.		
6.		
7.		
8.		
9.		
10.		

✏ PENCIL TOTALS

Cherub With Star
DX262 • 2 ½"
Issued: 1991 • Suspended: 1993
Market Value: $28

Cherub With Star
10445 • 5"
Issued: 1998 • Current
Market Value: $_____

Eager To Please
DX295 • 2 ⅛"
Issued: 1995 • Current
Market Value: $_____

The Finishing Touches
DS202 • 3 ½"
Issued: 1995 • Retired: 1995
Market Value: $20

1

Flying High
10137 • 2 ⅝″
Issued: 1997 • Current
Market Value: $_____

2

Golden Bell
10195 • 3 ½″
Issued: 1997 • Current
Market Value: $_____

3

Golden Candle
10198 • 4 ⅛″
Issued: 1997 • Current
Market Value: $_____

4

Golden Cross
10197 • 3 ⅜″
Issued: 1997 • Current
Market Value: $_____

5

Golden Heart
10194 • 3 ¼″
Issued: 1997 • Current
Market Value: $_____

6

Golden Snowflake
10196 • 4 ¼″
Issued: 1997 • Current
Market Value: $_____

7

Golden Wreath
10199 • 4″
Issued: 1997 • Current
Market Value: $_____

8

Hang My Stocking
DX291 • 2 ⅜″
Issued: 1995 • Current
Market Value: $_____

9

Holiday Express
10132 • 3″
Issued: 1997 • Current
Market Value: $_____

10

Holiday Hugs
10134 • 2 ¼″
Issued: 1997 • Current
Market Value: $_____

ORNAMENTS

	Price Paid	Value Of My Collection
1.		
2.		
3.		
4.		
5.		
6.		
7.		
8.		
9.		
10.		
✏ PENCIL TOTALS		

ORNAMENTS

(1)

I Can Read
DX297 • 1 ¾"
Issued: 1995 • Current
Market Value: $_____

(2)

Just For You
10135 • 2 ⅝"
Issued: 1997 • Current
Market Value: $_____

(3)

Kiss, Kiss
DX298 • 1 ⅞"
Issued: 1995 • Current
Market Value: $_____

(4)

Lamb
DX275 • 2 ½"
Issued: 1991 • Suspended: 1993
Market Value: $28

(5)

Nativity Ornament Set (set/6)
DX466 • Various
Issued: 1996 • Current
Market Value: $_____

(6)

Piggy
DX271 • 2 ½"
Issued: 1991 • Suspended: 1993
Market Value: $28

ORNAMENTS

	Price Paid	Value Of My Collection
1.		
2.		
3.		
4.		
5.		
6.		
7.		
8.		
9.		
10.		

✏ **PENCIL TOTALS**

(7)

Piggy Back Kitty
DX284 • 2"
Issued: 1994 • Current
Market Value: $_____

(8)

Poinsettia
DX292 • 1 ¾"
Issued: 1995 • Current
Market Value: $_____

(9)

Praying Cherub
DX261 • 2 ½"
Issued: 1991 • Suspended: 1993
Market Value: $28

(10)

Praying Cherub
10443 • 5"
Issued: 1998 • Current
Market Value: $_____

(1)

Raccoon
DX272 • 2 ½"
Issued: 1991 • Suspended: 1993
Market Value: $28

(2)

**Rainbow
Ornament Stand**
10089 • 6"
Issued: 1997 • Current
Market Value: $_____

(3)

**Santa In
Dreamsicle Land**
DS217 • 4 ½"
Issued: 1996 • Retired: 1996
Market Value: $15

(4)

Sleeping Cherub
10441 • 5"
Issued: 1998 • Current
Market Value: $_____

(5)

Squirrel
DX273 • 2 ½"
Issued: 1991 • Suspended: 1993
Market Value: $28

(6)

Star Of Wonder
10142 • 3 ½"
Issued: 1997 •Retired: 1997
Market Value: $15

(7)

Sucking My Thumb
DX293 • 2"
Issued: 1995 • Current
Market Value: $_____

(8)

Surprise Gift
DX296 • 1 ¾"
Issued: 1995 • Current
Market Value: $_____

(9)

Sweet Treat
10133 • 3 ⅛"
Issued: 1997 • Current
Market Value: $_____

(10)

Up All Night
DX294 • 1 ⅞"
Issued: 1995 • Current
Market Value: $_____

ORNAMENTS

	Price Paid	Value Of My Collection
1.		
2.		
3.		
4.		
5.		
6.		
7.		
8.		
9.		
10.		

✎ PENCIL TOTALS

ORNAMENTS

1

Pencil & Notepad Holder
10076 • 3 ¾"
Issued: 1997 • Current
Market Value: $_____

2

Bedtime Prayer
10214 • 9 ¼"
Issued: 1997 • Current
Market Value: $_____

3

Bless This House
DC177 • 5"
Issued: 1994 • Current
Market Value: $_____

4

Bunny Wall Plaque
5018 • 11 ½"
Issued: 1992 • Suspended: 1992
Market Value: N/E

5

Bunny Wall Plaque
5019 • 12 ½"
Issued: 1992 • Suspended: 1992
Market Value: N/E

6

Cherub Wall Plaque
5130 • 7"
Issued: 1992 • Suspended: 1992
Market Value: N/E

PENCIL HOLDERS

	Price Paid	Value Of My Collection
1.		

PLAQUES

2.		
3.		
4.		
5.		
6.		
7.		
8.		
9.		
10.		

7

Cherub Wall Plaque
5131 • 7"
Issued: 1992 • Suspended: 1992
Market Value: N/E

8

Heavenly Harp
10215 • 8 ¼"
Issued: 1997 • Current
Market Value: $_____

9

Join The Fun
10212 • 10 ½"
Issued: 1997 • Current
Market Value: $_____

10

Moonbeams
10213 • 11"
Issued: 1997 • Current
Market Value: $_____

✎ PENCIL TOTALS

1

Snuggle Blanket
10216 • 9"
Issued: 1997 • Current
Market Value: $_____

2

Starburst
10217 • 10"
Issued: 1997 • Current
Market Value: $_____

3

Watching Over You
DC176 • 5"
Issued: 1994 • Current
Market Value: $_____

4
New!

25th Anniversary Plate
10762 • 6 ¾"
Issued: 1999 • Current
Market Value: $_____

5
New!

50th Anniversary Plate
10763 • 6 ¾"
Issued: 1999 • Current
Market Value: $_____

6
New!

Anniversary Plate
10761 • 6 ¾"
Issued: 1999 • Current
Market Value: $_____

7

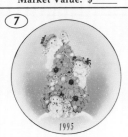

The Finishing Touches
DS200 • 8 ¼"
Issued: 1995 • Retired: 1995
Market Value: $45

8

**Santa In
Dreamsicle Land**
DS215 • 8 ¼"
Issued: 1996 • Retired: 1996
Market Value: $40

9

Star Of Wonder
10144 • 8"
Issued: 1997 • Retired: 1997
Market Value: $30

PLAQUES

	Price Paid	Value Of My Collection
1.		
2.		
3.		

PLATES

4.		
5.		
6.		
7.		
8.		
9.		

✎ **PENCIL TOTALS**

PLAQUES/PLATES

①

Cherub Bowl – Hearts
DC160 • 4"
Issued: 1994 • Suspended: 1997
Market Value: N/E

②

Cherub Bowl – Stars
DC161 • 4"
Issued: 1994 • Suspended: 1996
Market Value: $50

③

Potpourri Bunnies
DA117 • 4 ½"
Issued: 1994 • Suspended: 1996
Market Value: $20

④
New!

Potpourri/Candy Dish
10639 • 4 ⅜"
Issued: 1999 • Current
Market Value: $____

⑤

Potpourri Pals
DA118 • 3 ½"
Issued: 1994 • Suspended: 1996
Market Value: $20

⑥

Boxful Of Stars
DX224 • 3 ¾"
Issued: 1994 • Suspended: 1997
Market Value: N/E

POTPOURRI HOLDERS

	Price Paid	Value Of My Collection
1.		
2.		
3.		
4.		
5.		

STOCKING HOLDERS

6.		
7.		
8.		
9.		
10.		

✎ PENCIL TOTALS

⑦

Cherub With Moon
10460 • 3 ⅞"
Issued: 1998 • Current
Market Value: $____

⑧

Cherub With Train
10461 • 4 ⅛"
Issued: 1998 • Current
Market Value: $____

⑨

Cherub With Tree
10462 • 3 ½"
Issued: 1998 • Current
Market Value: $____

⑩

Sock Hop
DX222 • 3 ¾"
Issued: 1994 • Suspended: 1997
Market Value: N/E

1

**Stocking Holder
Christmas Tree**
DX221 • 5"
Issued: 1993 • Suspended: 1995
Market Value: $30

2

**Stocking Holder
Snowman**
DX219 • 5"
Issued: 1993 • Suspended: 1995
Market Value: $30

3

**Stocking Holder
Toboggan**
DX220 • 5"
Issued: 1993 • Suspended: 1995
Market Value: $30

4

Sweet Gingerbread
DX223 • 3 ¾"
Issued: 1994 • Suspended: 1997
Market Value: N/E

STOCKING HOLDERS

	Price Paid	Value Of My Collection
1.		
2.		
3.		
4.		

✏ **PENCIL TOTALS**

STOCKING HOLDERS

Dreamsicles® — FUTURE RELEASES

Use this page to record future Dreamsicles releases.

DREAMSICLES	Original Price	Status	Market Value	Year Purch.	Price Paid	Value of My Collection

PENCIL TOTALS

PRICE PAID	MARKET VALUE

TOTAL VALUE OF MY COLLECTION

Record the value of your collection here by adding the
pencil totals from the bottom of each Value Guide page.

DREAMSICLES

Page Number	Price Paid	Market Value
Page 35		
Page 36		
Page 37		
Page 38		
Page 39		
Page 40		
Page 41		
Page 42		
Page 43		
Page 44		
Page 45		
Page 46		
Page 47		
Page 48		
Page 49		
Page 50		
Page 51		
Page 52		
Page 53		
Page 54		
Page 55		
Page 56		
Page 57		
Page 58		
Page 59		
Page 60		
Page 61		
Page 62		
Page 63		
Page 64		
Page 65		
Page 66		
TOTAL		

DREAMSICLES

Page Number	Price Paid	Market Value
Page 67		
Page 68		
Page 69		
Page 70		
Page 71		
Page 72		
Page 73		
Page 74		
Page 75		
Page 76		
Page 77		
Page 78		
Page 79		
Page 80		
Page 81		
Page 82		
Page 83		
Page 84		
Page 85		
Page 86		
Page 87		
Page 88		
Page 89		
Page 90		
Page 91		
Page 92		
Page 93		
Page 94		
Page 95		
Page 96		
Page 97		
Page 98		
TOTAL		

Total Value

PAGE SUBTOTALS

PRICE PAID	MARKET VALUE

Total Value Of My Collection

Record the value of your collection here by adding the
pencil totals from the bottom of each Value Guide page.

DREAMSICLES		
Page Number	Price Paid	Market Value
Page 99		
Page 100		
Page 101		
Page 102		
Page 103		
Page 104		
Page 105		
Page 106		
Page 107		
Page 108		
Page 109		
Page 110		
Page 111		
Page 112		
Page 113		
Page 114		
Page 115		
Page 116		
Page 117		
Page 118		
Page 119		
Page 120		
Page 121		
Page 122		
Page 123		
Page 124		
Page 125		
Page 126		
Page 127		
Page 128		
Page 129		
Page 130		
TOTAL		

DREAMSICLES		
Page Number	Price Paid	Market Value
Page 131		
Page 132		
Page 133		
Page 134		
Page 135		
Page 136		
Page 137		
Page 138		
Page 139		
Page 140		
Page 141		
Page 142		
Page 143		
Page 144		
Page 145		
Page 146		
Page 147		
Page 148		
Page 149		
Page 150		
Page 151		
Page 152		
Page 153		
Page 154		
Page 155		
Page 156		
Page 157		
Page 158		
Page 159		
Page 160		
Page 161		
Page 162		
TOTAL		

	GRAND TOTALS	
Total Value		
	Price Paid	Market Value

*D*reamsicles started out far removed from the popular collectible status it enjoys today. Originally introduced as a gift line, the handcrafted figurines came with virtually no information – in fact, the first pieces were even released without names! Retailers had difficulty matching up boxes with figurines, and most people didn't realize the importance those boxes later would have in the collectibles world.

As the popularity of the cherubs and animals grew, Cast Art assigned names to the pieces. In the summer of 1994, identifying stickers with the piece's name and stock number were added to the bottoms of the figurines.

The first hint that the line might become a collectible came in 1992 when Cast Art began issuing figurines that were limited to 10,000 pieces. These early Limited Editions sold out within a year of their release, and the 1993 Limited Edition figurine "The Flying Lesson" became the fastest-selling Dreamsicles piece up to that point. As collectors scrambled to get these Limited Editions, prices began to increase on the secondary market.

WHAT IS THE SECONDARY MARKET?

The secondary market is a meeting ground where collectors can both buy and sell collectibles. It can be a valuable resource for acquiring hard-to-find pieces no longer available through retail stores. Secondary market pricing is based on three criteria: availability, condition and packaging.

HOW IT WORKS

For most collectible lines, a secondary market is born after pieces are retired – that is, removed from production and no longer available through retail stores. This means that once a retailer's stock is depleted, collectors have to look elsewhere to find that particular piece. When demand eventually surpasses the available supply, the retired piece increases in value on the secondary market. Limited editions and exclusive pieces typically draw the highest prices on the secondary market, as they were available for the shortest amount of time and to the fewest number of people.

THE CONDITION COUNTS

The value of any piece depends on its condition. Stray strokes of paint, chips, cracks and water damage can reduce the value of a figurine on the secondary market. There's nothing wrong with buying a piece that has been restored as long as you know that it has been repaired and you understand that its resale value will be decreased.

Packaging is nearly as important as the collectible itself when it comes to the secondary market. In the "real world," a box is just a box; but in the world of collectibles, boxes and packing sleeves take on an important new meaning. Not only are boxes perfect for storing and protecting your pieces, but many collectors will consider a piece without its original packaging to be "incomplete." These pieces will generally command a lower price on the secondary market.

SECONDARY MARKET SOURCES

Secondary market *exchange services* offer collectors the opportunity to list their pieces for sale with the prices they are asking. The exchange acts as a broker, or middleman, and charges a fee for any sale, generally between 10% and 20%. Exchanges usually issue a monthly or bi-weekly newsletter and charge a subscription or membership fee. Some exchanges generate daily listings.

The *Dreamsicles Club* provides a "Wish List" in its *ClubHouse* magazine where Club members may list

Dreamsicles for sale as well as the ones they want to buy.

The ***Internet*** is the newest method of accessing the secondary market. Here you will find web sites dedicated to Dreamsicles, including chat rooms and bulletin boards where you can share information with other collectors and access up-to-the-minute price listings. Auction sites allow you to sell and bid on collectibles, as well as establish contacts with people who share your love of Dreamsicles.

Many ***magazines*** and ***newspapers*** have "Swap and Sell" sections for collectors. Check the "Antiques & Collectibles" listings in the classified advertisements, but keep in mind that because newspapers reach a general audience and not collectors specifically, this approach may not be as quick and effective as some of the other options.

Your local ***retailer*** may also be able to help you. While most retailers aren't directly involved with the secondary market, they may be able to refer you to other collectors who are looking to buy, sell or trade pieces, or they may sponsor secondary market collector shows as a service to customers.

TIMING IT RIGHT

Sales on the secondary market typically slow down in the summer and pick up as the holidays approach. Because demand – and prices – increase later in the year, you may prefer to sell late in the year and buy at another time. There really is no right or wrong time to buy or sell; it all depends on how much you're willing to pay for a piece that you want to add to your collection.

Not every piece will soar in value, so if your sole reason to collect Dreamsicles is for the investment, you may be disappointed. You're much better off doing it for the smiles they bring!

PRODUCTION

1. Artist Kristin Haynes dreams up new ideas for her popular and much loved cherubs and animals and transforms them into prototype sculptures at her farmhouse in rural Idaho.

2. At factories in California and Mexico, Cast Art's skilled artisans use the prototypes to create molds that are injected with a special formulation of natural gypsum material.

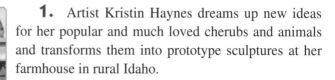

3. When the drying process is complete, the figurine is removed from the mold and hand finished to remove any imperfections caused by the molding process.

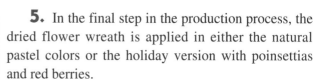

4. Delicate hand painting produces the subtle pastel shading and expressive eyes characteristic of each Dreamsicles piece. Every figurine is signature stamped.

5. In the final step in the production process, the dried flower wreath is applied in either the natural pastel colors or the holiday version with poinsettias and red berries.

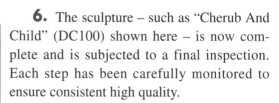

6. The sculpture – such as "Cherub And Child" (DC100) shown here – is now complete and is subjected to a final inspection. Each step has been carefully monitored to ensure consistent high quality.

7. Most of the finished sculptures are individually packaged. Each figurine is inserted into a recycled foam liner for protection then packaged in a special Dreamsicles box.

PACKAGING

Dreamsicles figurines come packaged in a protective foam liner inside a colorful gift box. New packaging designs were phased into production in 1998. These boxes feature the Dreamsicles logo and an image of a smiling cherub, with additional designs for holiday, limited edition and special Club Members-Only pieces. Because collectibles typically command higher prices on the secondary market if accompanied by their original boxes, you should retain all packaging when purchasing your Dreamsicles pieces.

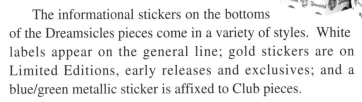

The informational stickers on the bottoms of the Dreamsicles pieces come in a variety of styles. White labels appear on the general line; gold stickers are on Limited Editions, early releases and exclusives; and a blue/green metallic sticker is affixed to Club pieces.

In 1998, Cast Art randomly placed orange pumpkin stickers on the bottom of 2,000 Halloween figurines, replacing the usual round, white labels. Collectors should have a lot of fun looking for these specially-marked figurines, which were shipped throughout the country!

PRICING

Dreamsicles typically range in price from $7 to $30 for the smaller pieces; from $30 to $100 for the larger, more detailed figurines; and from $100 to $150 for the limited edition pieces.

CARE, CLEANING AND REPAIR

*Y*our Dreamsicles are all set up in a perfect display, but they're getting a little dusty. How do you clean these fragile little figurines? Cast Art Industries offers the following care, cleaning and repair tips.

For routine dusting of your collection, use a small, stiff – but soft – paintbrush. The bristles can reach the dust in the figurine's tiny crevices, which can be difficult to reach. Some collectors prefer to use a bristled vacuum cleaner attachment or a hair dryer to blow dust off of their valuables. When using a hair dryer, make sure to set it on "high air, low heat," so as not to melt any paint on the figurine.

For routine cleaning, lightly dust the figurines with baking soda. Let the baking soda set for about five minutes to absorb all the skin oils and dust. Then, very carefully buff the baking soda off with a dry, soft cloth. Be careful not to rub harshly, as scrubbing will remove the paint.

And what about that delicate wreath that adorns each of Kristin Haynes cherubs? Cast Art offers a "Dreamsicles T.L.C. Repair Kit" that contains all the materials necessary to repair the floral wreaths of approximately 20 Dreamsicles figurines. The kit includes a soft dusting brush, glue gun, ribbon, flowers and grass and can be purchased through your local retailer or through the Dreamsicles Club.

When insuring your collection, there are three major points to consider:

1. Know your coverage. Collectibles are typically included in homeowner's or renter's insurance policies. Ask your agent if your policy covers fire, theft, floods, hurricanes earthquakes and damage or breakage through routine handling. Also, ask if your policy covers claims at "current replacement value" – the amount it would cost to replace items if they were damaged, lost or stolen – which is extremely important since the secondary market value of some pieces may well exceed their original retail prices.

2. Document your collection. In the event of a loss, your insurance company will need proof of your collection and its value. Ask your insurance agent what information is acceptable. Keep receipts and an inventory of your collection in a different location, such as a safe deposit box, so they are accessible in case of a fire. Include the purchase date, price paid, size, issue year, edition limit, special markings and secondary market value for each piece. List the boxes you have, too, as they are important factors in determining the value of your collection.

> Many companies will accept a reputable secondary market price guide – such as the Collector's Value Guide™ – as a valid source for determining your collection's value.

3. Weigh the risk. To determine the coverage you need, calculate how much it would cost to replace your collection and compare it to the total amount your current policy would pay. If the amount of insurance does not cover your collection, ask your agent about adding a Personal Articles Floater or a Fine Arts Floater or "rider" to your policy, or insuring your collection under a separate policy. As with all insurance, you must weigh the risk of loss against the cost of additional coverage.

Display Tips

*D*isplaying your Dreamsicles is the fun part and there's no shortage of decorating options! Deciding how to showcase your pieces – whether you collect cherubs, animals or other Dreamiscles family members – can help bring your collection alive.

One of the more important things to remember is to protect your collection from harm – which could be in the form of your favorite little nephew or granddaughter, your curious kitty or even the ravages of daily dust and sunlight. Most collectors opt to place their cherished cherubs inside curio cabinets or on shelves. Some collectors even opt to place their most valuable pieces inside protective plastic boxes.

One of the best ways to showcase a Dreamsicles collection is to display the pieces in a themed setting. A fun way to do this is to think of monthly and holiday events that could serve as grouping ideas for your pieces. Your local craft supply store can be a wonderful place to discover ideas for scenes and accessories.

SPRING

The first signs of spring remind us to "lighten and brighten." Your Dreamsicles will coordinate beautifully with colorful Easter grass, small baskets of jelly beans or eggs, and small pots of delicate flowers such as daffodils, pansies and daisies. The wide variety of Dreamsicles bunnies and Easter-themed pieces provide an array of choices to include with your display.

SUMMER

The Fourth of July holiday can inspire great patriotic display ideas. You can display the 1999 pieces "Soldier Boy," "Sailor Boy" and "A Few Good Men" with some of Dad's army medals and memorabilia, or with miniature ships and planes. A backdrop of patriotic print fabric or an American flag would be an appropriate choice.

FALL

October brings Halloween and an excuse to decorate in black and orange colors – a great way to show off the new

Miralite™ Dreamsicles! Faux spider webs with black plastic spiders, a full moon hanging over the witches and goblins, a straw broom, a miniature witch's hat, Halloween votives and a stuffed black cat make for a frightful scene!

WINTER

To showcase figurines with a wintry weather theme, vary the height of the display with blocks of wood draped with a

snow blanket, add some appropriately sized sisal trees and a small mirror for a frozen pond. Now place your favorite winter-themed Dreamsicles, snowmen and Santas in their very own winter wonderland!

Birthday

Happy First Birthday (10701), Happy Second Birthday (10702), Happy Third Birthday (10703)

Easter

The Easter Story (10737), The Easter Trail (10740), Easter Colors (10738)

Mother's Day

I Love You Mom (10706), Mama's Little Helper (10708), Moms Are A Gift (10682)

New Baby

Babies Are Precious (10683), An Angel's Watching Over You (10684), Someone Cares (10674)

Valentine's Day

Be My Valentine (10642), Declaration Of Love (10635), Love Poems (10637)

Wedding

Wedding Cake Box (10758), Cake Topper (10757), Bride & Groom Candlestick (10759)

bas-relief — sculptural process that leaves a raised design.

collectible — anything that is "able to be collected," such as figurines and dolls. Even *old keys* can be considered a "collectible," but generally a true collectible is something that increases in value over time.

current — piece that is in current production and available in retail stores.

early release — piece released as a "special preview" to selected stores before its scheduled introduction into the general collection.

exchange — secondary market service that lists pieces that collectors wish to buy or sell. The exchange works as a middleman and usually requires a commission.

exclusive — figurine made especially for, and available only through, a specific store.

Gift Creations Concepts (GCC) — a syndicated catalog group for retail stores nationwide. Exclusive pieces and early releases are commonly available through these retailers.

Hydrastone — specially formulated natural gypsum material out of which most Dreamsicles are made.

International Collectible Exposition (I.C.E.) — national collectible shows held annually in June at Rosemont, Illinois and in April alternating between California and New Jersey.

issue year — for Dreamsicles, the year that a piece becomes available in the general collection.

limited edition (LE) — a piece that is scheduled for a predetermined production quantity or time.

Members-Only piece — special item only available for purchase by members of the Dreamsicles Club.

mid-year introductions — pieces announced in June as follow-ups to the major January introductions.

mint condition — piece offered on the secondary market that is in "like-new" condition.

Miralite™ — high-gloss metallic finish available on a selection of holiday figurines and ornaments.

new introductions — new pieces announced in January.

open edition — piece with no predetermined limit on time or size of production.

Parade Of Gifts — a syndicated catalog group for retail stores nationwide. Exclusive pieces and early releases are commonly available through these retailers.

primary market — the conventional purchasing process, buying from retailers at issue price.

resin — thick liquid used to bind together different materials for the production of a collectible.

retired — piece taken out of production by Cast Art Industries, never to be made again.

secondary market — source for buying and selling retired and hard-to-find collectibles. It can include newspaper ads, collector newsletters, the Internet and "swap & sells."

suspended — piece removed from production that may return in the future.

swap & sell — event where collectors buy, sell or trade items.

Symbol Of Membership figurine — special gift to collectors joining or renewing their memberships to the Dreamsicles Club.

variations — items with color, design or text changes from the "original" pieces, whether intentional or not. Some changes may affect the value of a piece on the secondary market.

– Key –

All Dreamsicles pieces are listed below in numerical order by stock number. The first number refers to the piece's location within the Value Guide section and the second to the box in which it is pictured on that page.

NUMERICAL INDEX

NUMERICAL INDEX

NUMERICAL INDEX

– Key –

All Dreamsicles pieces are listed below in alphabetical order. The first number refers to the piece's location within the Value Guide section and the second to the box in which it is pictured on that page.

Alphabetical Index

ALPHABETICAL INDEX

ALPHABETICAL INDEX

ALPHABETICAL INDEX

ALPHABETICAL INDEX

ACKNOWLEDGEMENTS

CheckerBee Publishing would like to thank Mark & Kim Wendelsdorf, John & Val SoRelle, Tracy Metzler, Michelle Payne, Norma Staley and the many other people who contributed their valuable time to assist us with this book. Special thanks to the great people at Cast Art Industries.